WITHDRAWN

INTRODUCING
ISSUES
WITH

OPPOSING VIEWPOINTS®

ALCOHOL

Other books in the Introducing Issues
with Opposing Viewpoints series:

INTRODUCING ISSUES WITH

OPPOSING VIEWPOINTS®

ALCOHOL

Scott Barbour, *Book Editor*

Bruce Glassman, *Vice President*
Bonnie Szumski, *Publisher, Series Editor*
Helen Cothran, *Managing Editor*

OPPOSING VIEWPOINTS® SERIES

GREENHAVEN PRESS

An imprint of Thomson Gale, a part of The Thomson Corporation

THOMSON

GALE

Detroit • New York • San Francisco • San Diego • New Haven, Conn. • Waterville, Maine • London • Munich

© 2006 Thomson Gale, a part of The Thomson Corporation.

Thomson and Star Logo are trademarks and Gale and Greenhaven Press are registered trademarks used herein under license.

For more information, contact
Greenhaven Press
27500 Drake Rd.
Farmington Hills, MI 48331-3535
Or you can visit our Internet site at http://www.gale.com

LIBRARY OF CONGRESS CATALOGING-IN-PUBLICATION DATA
Alcohol / Scott Barbour, book editor.
p.cm. — (Introducing issues with opposing viewpoints)
Includes bibliographical references and index.
ISBN 0-7377-3219-9 (lib. : alk. paper)
1. Alcoholism—United States. 2. Youth—Alcohol use—United States. 3. Minors—Alcohol use—United States. 4. Drunk driving—United States. I. Barbour, Scott, 1963– . II. Series.
HV5292.A379 2006
362.292'0973—dc22
2005040327

Printed in the United States of America

CONTENTS

Chapter 3: How Can Drunk Driving Be Reduced?

Indulging in a wide spectrum of ideas, beliefs, and perspectives is a critical cornerstone of democracy. After all, it is often debates over differences of opinion, such as whether to legalize abortion, how to treat prisoners, or when to enact the death penalty that shape our society and drive it forward. Such diversity of thought is frequently regarded as the hallmark of a healthy and civilized culture. As the Reverend Clifford Schutjer of the First Congregational Church in Mansfield, Ohio, declared in a 2001 sermon, "Surrounding oneself with only like-minded people, restricting what we listen to or read only to what we find agreeable is irresponsible. Refusing to entertain doubts once we make up our minds is a subtle but deadly form of arrogance." With this advice in mind, Introducing Issues with Opposing Viewpoints books aim to open readers' minds to the critically divergent views that comprise our world's most important debates.

Introducing Issues with Opposing Viewpoints simplifies for students the enormous and often overwhelming mass of material now available via print and electronic media. Collected in every volume is an array of opinions that capture the essence of a particular controversy or topic. Introducing Issues with Opposing Viewpoints books embody the spirit of nineteenth-century journalist Charles A. Dana's axiom: "Fight for your opinions, but do not believe that they contain the whole truth, or the only truth." Absorbing such contrasting opinions teaches students to analyze the strength of an argument and compare it to its opposition. From this process readers can inform and strengthen their own opinions, or be exposed to new information that will change their minds. Introducing Issues with Opposing Viewpoints is a mosaic of different voices. The authors are statesmen, pundits, academics, journalists, corporations, and ordinary people who have felt compelled to share their experiences and ideas in a public forum. Their words have been collected from newspapers, journals, books, speeches, interviews, and the Internet, the fastest growing body of opinionated material in the world.

Introducing Issues with Opposing Viewpoints shares many of the well-known features of its critically acclaimed parent series, Opposing Viewpoints. The articles are presented in a pro/con format, allowing readers to absorb divergent perspectives side by side. Active reading questions preface each viewpoint, requiring the student to approach the material thoughtfully and carefully. Useful charts, graphs, and cartoons supplement each article. A thorough introduction provides readers with crucial background on an issue. An annotated bibliography points the reader toward articles, books, and Web sites that contain additional information on the topic. An appendix of organizations to contact contains a wide variety of charities, nonprofit organizations, political groups, and private enterprises that each hold a position on the issue at hand. Finally, a comprehensive index allows readers to locate content quickly and efficiently.

Introducing Issues with Opposing Viewpoints is also significantly different from Opposing Viewpoints. As the series title implies, its presentation will help introduce students to the concept of opposing viewpoints, and learn to use this material to aid in critical writing and debate. The series' four-color, accessible format makes the books attractive and inviting to readers of all levels. In addition, each viewpoint has been carefully edited to maximize a reader's understanding of the content. Short but thorough viewpoints capture the essence of an argument. A substantial, thought-provoking essay question placed at the end of each viewpoint asks the student to further investigate the issues raised in the viewpoint, compare and contrast two authors' arguments, or consider how one might go about forming an opinion on the topic at hand. Each viewpoint contains sidebars that include at-a-glance information and handy statistics. A Facts About section located in the back of the book further supplies students with relevant facts and figures.

Following in the tradition of the Opposing Viewpoints series, Greenhaven Press continues to provide readers with invaluable exposure to the controversial issues that shape our world. As John Stuart Mill once wrote: "The only way in which a human being can make some approach to knowing the whole of a subject is by hearing what can be said about it by persons of every variety of opinion and studying all modes in which it can be looked at by every character of mind. No wise man ever acquired his wisdom in any mode but this." It is to this principle that Introducing Issues with Opposing Viewpoints books are dedicated.

INTRODUCTION

"Alcohol is both a tonic and a poison."

—Harvard School of Public Health

In 2001, in Corvallis, Oregon, fourteen-year-old Tamara Wardles died of alcohol poisoning after downing eight vodka drinks in twenty-five minutes. The same year in Miami, after spending an afternoon drinking with a friend, seventeen-year-old Carla Wagner struck and killed a sixteen-year-old rollerblader before crashing into a tree. She was subsequently sentenced to three to six years in prison. In September 2004, eighteen-year-old Lynn "Gordie" Bailey, a freshman at the University of Boulder in Colorado, died after drinking a large amount of whiskey and wine during a fraternity initiation celebration.

These are just a few examples of the devastating effects of alcohol. In each case, alcohol ended at least one life and sent ripples of grief through families and communities. As tragic as they are, stories such as these are far from rare. Indeed, statistics reveal that the consumption of alcohol is widespread in American society. According to the Substance Abuse and Mental Health Services Administration (SAMHSA), a division of the U.S. government that studies mental health issues, about half of all Americans over the age of twelve (or 119 million people) report having at least one drink in the past thirty days. One-fifth of Americans report that they have participated in binge drinking—that is, drinking five or more drinks on the same occasion—in the past thirty

A student sits in a car with crashed motorcycles piled on its hood to expose the dangers of drunk driving.

days. And 6.8 percent of Americans report heavy drinking, which is defined as binge drinking five or more times within the past thirty days.

The rate of drinking among teens is especially alarming. According to SAMHSA, 29 percent of youths between twelve and twenty report drinking in the past month. Over 19 percent report binge drinking, and 6.1 percent report heavy drinking. Older teens drink more than younger youths. According to Monitoring the Future, an ongoing study being conducted by the University of Maryland, over 70 percent of twelfth graders report drinking in the past year. In contrast, 60 percent of tenth graders and 38 percent of eighth graders report drinking in the past year.

All of this drinking can have catastrophic consequences. The National Institute of Alcohol Abuse and Alcoholism estimates that nearly 14 million Americans—one in thirteen adults—either abuses alcohol or is an alcoholic. Alcohol abuse and alcoholism can wreak havoc on families, careers, and personal relationships. In addition,

Participating in a demonstration against drunk driving, a woman holds up a photograph of her daughter who was killed in 2001 in a drunk-driving incident.

Despite the inherent dangers of alcohol abuse, millions of people consume alcohol with no adverse effects.

heavy drinking can cause serious health problems, including liver disease, heart damage, and cancer. The abuse of alcohol also has wider societal impacts: Alcohol is involved in one-fourth of violent crimes such as rape, murder, and spousal abuse. And drunk-driving accidents kill more than seventeen thousand people a year.

Despite its potential to inflict great harm on individuals and society, alcohol is a legal drug that is enjoyed by millions of people. In fact, most of the estimated 119 million U.S. drinkers experience no adverse results due to their consumption of alcohol. As stated by radio commentator Dennis Prager, "Countless good people drink without the slightest ill effect on themselves or on others. Indeed, when consumed prudently, wine, alcohol and beer can add a bit to the sum total of human happiness." Moreover, alcohol can also improve health. Experts agree that moderate drinking—defined as two drinks per day for men and one drink per day for women—reduces the risk of heart disease.

It is this double-edged-sword quality of alcohol—its capacity for good as well as great harm—that creates the debate over alcohol and how to curb its devastation. Many medical and public health experts want to protect people from themselves by tightening up regulations on alcohol. Among other solutions, they call for raising taxes on alcohol, stricter penalties for drunk driving, and restrictions on alcohol advertising. "The intensity of efforts to prevent alcohol problems must match the enormity of the crisis," states the Marin Institute, one of several nonprofit organizations devoted to this cause.

Opponents of these measures are rather cynical about their impact. They point out that, because it is legal to drink alcohol, there is really no way to prevent alcohol abuse. Even in states, such as New Mexico, where the buying and selling of alcohol is strictly regulated, the laws have had little effect on the alcoholism rate.

The widely divergent views of alcohol proponents and reformers suggest that, on the topic of alcohol, Americans are sharply divided. These contrasting perspectives are illustrated in *Introducing Issues with Opposing Viewpoints: Alcohol,* which contains the following chapters: Is Alcohol Harmful to Society? How Can Underage Drinking Be Prevented? How Can Drunk Driving Be Reduced? Throughout these chapters, authors debate the harmfulness of alcohol and various solutions to the problems associated with its use and abuse.

CHAPTER 1

Is Alcohol Harmful to Society?

Alcohol Is Harmful to Society

Deborah Williams

"Alcohol . . . is abused by some 14 million Americans and contributes to the deaths of 100,000 each year."

In the following viewpoint Deborah Williams argues that alcohol causes many problems in American society and around the world. She contends that alcoholism is a major health problem that ruins lives and burdens the economy. Rates of alcohol abuse among young people and the elderly are particularly disturbing, she writes. According to Williams, the negative consequences of alcohol abuse include alcohol-related illnesses, drunk-driving accidents, suicide, and violent crime. Deborah Williams is a freelance writer in New York State.

AS YOU READ, CONSIDER THE FOLLOWING QUESTIONS:

1. What fact does the death of Christine Gallagher demonstrate, according to her father?
2. Why is alcoholism among the elderly hard to detect, according to Williams?
3. How many children live with a parent who is dependent on alcohol or illegal drugs, according to the statistics cited by the author?

A teenage girl almost drowns in a backyard Amherst pool. A woman drives a pickup truck the wrong way down an interstate highway, hitting a car head-on and killing a father and his 12-year-old daughter.

Mayhem breaks out in the aftermath of a European soccer match in Belgium.

A university fraternity hazing turns to tragedy when an Orchard Park student lapses into a coma and dies.

A lonely widower falls and breaks his hip and is unable to move until rescued by a neighbor.

These incidents span continents. They involve young and old. What they and countless similar happenings are about is simple. Unfortunately, their true nature is often ignored or hidden.

They are all about alcohol.

The Enemy: Booze

The late Caroline Knapp, author of *Drinking: A Love Story*, a memoir of her personal struggle to overcome alcoholism, summed it up well:

"We have seen this enemy time and again, and the only thing more troubling than its savagery and frequency is our reluctance to call it by its proper name: booze."

Firefighters hose down the charred remains of a car destroyed in a drunk-driving accident. Automobile accidents are just one type of problem caused by alcohol abuse.

In an essay she concluded:

"Tobacco has been vilified in this culture. The war on drugs is waged on illegal narcotics: crack, heroin, cocaine. Ecstasy is now enjoying its place in the spotlight, the social ill du jour. Alcohol, meanwhile, is abused by some 14 million Americans and contributes to the deaths of 100,000 each year. Our culture bottles it, buys it, uses it, glamorizes it, needs it. Perhaps we should start being honest about it, too."

Dick Gallagher, executive director of Alcohol and Drug Dependency Services, knows first hand that alcoholism can affect any family. Ten years ago his only daughter Christine, 24, was just six credits short of receiving her degree at Buffalo [New York] State College. After a drinking binge, she came home, put her car in the garage with the engine running and was found dead by her family.

> **FAST FACT**
>
> Heavy drinkers are ten times more likely to get cancer than those who drink moderately or not at all. Heavy drinking can also cause brain damage, high blood pressure and cholesterol levels, an enlarged heart, and diseases of the liver and pancreas.

"We had arranged her treatment at Bry-Lin Hospital for her alcohol problems when she was 18," he explained. "She responded to treatment and did well for quite a while, but alcoholism is a chronic disease and certainly relapses can happen. Her suicide showed that no one is immune from the ravages of this disease." . . .

"People and governments do not understand the magnitude of the effect of alcoholism on the criminal justice and health care systems," he said. "The stigma still exists. Alcohol treatment is still restricted, and most people have limited benefit packages even when they seek treatment. The media and the advertising industry still glamorize drinking and alcohol companies spend millions to attract new drinkers."

Two years ago the World Health Organization called for an international review of alcohol marketing to youth. In the United States some health groups have seized on recent controversial beer ads, including one featuring women wrestling in wet cement, as proof that marketers aim their advertising at teenagers.

"You look at them, and it's all about the sex, attractiveness, popularity, independence, adventure, rebellion—everything an adolescent wants to be doing or is doing," said George Hacker, director for the alcohol policies project at the Center for Science in the Public Interest in Washington. . . .

Reports Reveal Abuse Is Rampant

The National Center on Addiction and Substance Abuse at Columbia University recently released a report stating that underage drinkers account for nearly 20 percent of the alcohol consumed in the United States each year. This figure represents $22.5 billion in sales. The report also said that excessive drinking by adults—consumption of more than two alcoholic drinks, including wine and beer, daily—amounted to 30.4 percent of sales, or $34.4 billion.

The latest survey by the Centers for Disease Control and Prevention found that 30 percent of all high school students had engaged in episodic heavy drinking within the last 30 days, meaning they each had five or more drinks in a row one or more occasions during the month. And the average age at which young people start drinking has dropped to 14.

Source: Asay. © by Charles Asay. Reproduced by permission.

Alcohol is a central part of many college students' spring break celebrations, such as the traditional gathering in Daytona Beach, Florida, pictured here.

This is spring break time, the annual rite for many college and even some high school students. In addition to frolicking in the sun, spring break has turned into a series of drinking binges among many students. According to a study in the *Journal of American College Health,* the average male has 18 alcoholic drinks per day and the average female has 10 drinks per day during their spring holiday. Half of all males and 40 percent of females on spring break drank to the point of vomiting or passing out a least once.

Alcoholism is particularly insidious among young people and the elderly, in part because the symptoms are not easily recognized until the affected person becomes truly alcohol dependent.

Experts call alcohol abuse by the elderly a hidden epidemic. The symptoms often mimic or are masked by common physical and mental infirmities of aging. Alcohol can cause dangerous interactions with medications that are more commonly taken by older people. Older people and their relatives are often in denial about the extent and effects of their drinking habits. A serious fall or an auto accident can be attributed to being old rather than the truth: having a drinking problem.

"Alcoholism is clearly a major health care issue which needs more attention," says Gerald Connors, Ph.D., executive director of the Research Institute on Addictions. . . . "It is a very dangerous substance for some people, and yet it doesn't seem to capture the anxieties of the public or of parents." . . .

Debating the Health Benefits of Alcohol

A January report in the *New England Journal of Medicine* points out that alcohol is the sharpest double-edged sword in medicine. The report stirred up a long-standing controversy over alcohol's health benefits by drawing the conclusion that a drink a day is often the best nonprescription way to prevent heart attacks.

Thirty years ago health officials were so uncomfortable with this idea that a federal agency tried to suppress early data on alcohol's beneficial effects. Experts in the field of alcoholism point out that denial is one of the hallmarks of the disease, and people with alcohol problems will likely use the latest studies as an additional excuse to drink. Of course the ravages of excessive alcohol are all too visible, and the benefits are largely invisible—disease simply does not happen.

An accompanying *New England Journal of Medicine* editorial by Ira J. Goldberg, M.D., stated that "there is insufficient information to encourage patients who do not drink alcohol to start—if alcohol were a newly discovered drug (instead of a drink dating back to the dawn of human history), we can be sure that no pharmaceutical company would develop it to prevent cardiovascular disease. Nor would many physicians use a therapy that might reduce the rate of myocardial infarction (heart attack) by 25 to 50 percent, but that would result in thousands of additional deaths per year due to cancer, motor vehicle accidents and liver disease." . . .

Mind-Boggling Statistics

The statistics regarding alcohol are mind-boggling, but they seem somehow to have lost their ability to elicit outrage. According to the National Council on Alcoholism and Drug Dependence:

76 million Americans have been exposed to alcoholism or problem drinking through a spouse, sibling, child or other relative.

More than 9 million children live with a parent dependent on alcohol and/or illicit drugs.

One-quarter of all emergency room admissions, one-third of all suicides, and more than half of all homicides and incidents of domestic violence are alcohol related.

Heavy drinking contributes to illness in each of the top three causes of death—heart disease, cancer and stroke.

Almost half of all traffic fatalities are alcohol related.

Between 48 and 64 percent of people who die in fires have blood alcohol levels indicating intoxication.

Alcohol and drug abuse costs the American economy an estimated $276 billion per year in lost productivity, health care expenditures, crime, motor vehicle crashes and other conditions.

And yet the drinks continue to flow.

EVALUATING THE AUTHORS' ARGUMENTS:

In the viewpoint you just read, Deborah Williams begins with several anecdotes describing tragedies caused by alcohol. In the next viewpoint, Michael Judge begins with a quote from Winston Churchill regarding his enjoyment of alcohol. Which opening more powerfully introduces the author's argument, and why?

The Harms of Alcohol Are Exaggerated

Michael Judge

"Many societies have positive experiences with alcohol."

In the following viewpoint, Michael Judge criticizes efforts to reduce alcohol use in America, including limits on advertising and promotions. He accuses the people and groups behind these attempts of overstating the harms of alcohol while ignoring the health benefits of moderate drinking. According to Judge, these anti-alcohol activists are mistaken to view liquor simply as a moral and social problem. In fact, he says, drinking is a custom that is widely accepted in societies around the world. Michael Judge is an assistant features editor at the *Wall Street Journal*.

AS YOU READ, CONSIDER THE FOLLOWING QUESTIONS:
1. How are college towns attempting to lower alcohol use, as reported by Judge?
2. How do drinking rates in the United States compare with those in Europe, according to the author?
3. What lesson can be learned from Europe about the effects of teaching moderation regarding alcohol, according to the author?

L et us begin with my favorite Churchill quote, and one that is terribly apropos given our irrational fear of intoxicating spirits:

Upon being told by Ibn Saud [the king of Saudi Arabia] that the king's religious beliefs forbade the use of tobacco and liquor, the great man didn't miss a beat. "I must point out that my rule of life," Churchill intoned, "prescribes as an absolutely sacred rite smoking cigars and also the drinking of alcohol before, after and if need be during all meals and in the intervals between them."

Oh, for a measure of this honesty and eloquence in today's politicians. For a nation that is more comfortable with its president choking on a pretzel than washing one down with a Budweiser, Churchill's words are an assault on our temperate sensibilities. In our 12-step society we find it hard to tolerate, let alone venerate, such a brash celebration of "vice."

A New Temperance Movement

Which brings us to the issue at hand: While a brawl over how fast a Guinness should be poured is heating up across the Atlantic, a new temperance movement is sweeping across America.

Local governments, most notably in college towns, are banning happy hours, two-for-ones, dollar pitchers and a host of other insidious drink specials at an alarming rate—never mind the fact that overall drinking among Americans, including college students, is declining.

Iowa City, Iowa, for example, home to the University of Iowa, my alma mater, enacted an ordinance in August [2002] making it illegal to sell more than two servings of alcohol to one person at a time; alas, two-for-one and all-you-can-drink specials were also banned.

It gets worse. The American Medical Association is calling for local ordinances against "reckless marketing practices" that target students with ads for boozy events like Barenaked Ladies concerts and spring-break packages to Boca Raton. And college boards are listening. Berkeley is just one of the many campuses where events sponsored by alcohol and tobacco companies are no-nos.

Much of this hysteria has to do with the state of perpetual alarm trumpeted by groups like Columbia University's National Center on Addiction and Substance Abuse. Last month [February 2002] NCASA shocked us with its announcement that "underage" drinkers between 12 and 20 consume 25% of all alcoholic beverages downed in the U.S. That's enough wine coolers to float a battleship.

Problem is, it wasn't true. NCASA President Joseph Califano Jr. acknowledged the true figure was closer to 11%, and most of that was done by young adults between the ages of 18 and 20. Underage? Yes. But old enough to vote and serve in the military—and a little over 10 years ago, old enough to drink in some states.

In an effort to reduce drinking among students, college towns have passed new laws regulating alcohol. Here a police officer enforces a ban on open alcohol containers on public property.

Source: Wright. © 2003 by Cagle Cartoons, Inc. Reproduced by permission.

Booze Is Seen as Immoral

Underage drinkers aren't the only ones that latter-day prohibitionists want to protect from Big Booze. [In March 2002] . . . NBC executives threw in the bar towel and reversed their decision to become the first TV network to air liquor commercials, even though guidelines for the ads were similar to those for beer and wine: The commercials would air only at night and only after the advertiser had aired four months of "social responsibility" ads stressing designated drivers, moderation and the like.

You can't blame NBC for folding, given the criticism; but it's too bad the broadcasters couldn't have stood by their guns. Fact is, we consume less alcohol than our counterparts in Britain, New Zealand or Australia, and just half that of Ireland, Spain, Germany or France.

But that hasn't stopped us from joining Alcoholics Anonymous at far greater rates than people abroad. The U.S. has more than 160 alcohol-related support groups per million citizens; that's nearly 10 times the number in most industrialized countries, and 20 times the number in France. As Mark Steyn wrote last May in the *Daily Telegraph* of London—after Jenna Bush's arrest for attempting to purchase a margarita—"America isn't addicted to alcohol, it's addicted to alcohol support groups."

The problem is that many Americans see boozing as somehow immoral and not a salutary part of social mores. Studies by the Berkeley Alcohol Research Group and a host of others find that nations that teach children moderation over abstinence, such as France, Spain and Italy, may have higher overall rates of alcohol consumption, but far lower rates of alcoholism and alcohol-related disease.

No one in his right mind would encourage so-called binge drinking among young people—or older ones either. The point is that acknowledging the social and, yes, health benefits of moderate, responsible drinking is a surer way to guard against excess than preaching abstention. As Brown University's Dwight D. Heath argues in his informative book, *Drinking Occasions: Comparative Perspectives on Alcohol and Culture,* many societies have positive experiences with alcohol that don't necessarily coincide with lower levels of consumption. In other words, Churchill wasn't alone in thinking of drink as his "sacred rite."

I'm by no means proposing that President Bush follow Frederick the Great's example by outlawing coffee and demanding that Americans drink nothing but beer, though the thought has crossed my mind. But if forced to choose between the Koran's teaching that there's "a devil in every berry of the grape" and Thomas Aquinas's saying that "Sorrow can be alleviated by good sleep, a bath and a glass of wine," I would have to side with the Angelic Doctor. To do otherwise would be bad not just for the soul, but for the body as well.

EVALUATING THE AUTHOR'S ARGUMENTS:

In the viewpoint you just read, Michael Judge writes that alcohol opponents are part of a "new temperance movement." What do you think he is trying to accomplish by using this label? Do you think he is successful?

Teen Alcohol Abuse Is a Serious Problem

National Research Council and the Institute of Medicine

"Public concern about teenage alcohol use has not been remotely commensurate with the magnitude of the problem."

The National Research Council and the Institute of Medicine are institutions that provide the public with advice about science and health policy. In 2004 these organizations collaborated to produce a report on the topic of underage drinking. The report surveyed the extent of the problem and made several recommendations designed to prevent the abuse of alcohol by young people. Its recommendations included increasing taxes on alcohol, implementing a national media campaign to educate adults about the problem, and reducing youths' exposure to media messages promoting and condoning alcohol use. In the following viewpoint, excerpted from the introduction to the report, the authors argue that underage drinking is a widespread problem that is not getting the attention it warrants.

National Research Council and the Institute of Medicine, *Reducing Underage Drinking: A Collective Responsibility.* Washington, DC: National Academies Press, 2004. Copyright © 2004 by the National Academy of Sciences, courtesy of the National Academies Press, Washington, DC. Reproduced with permission.

AS YOU READ, CONSIDER THE FOLLOWING QUESTIONS:
1. What consequences of underage drinking does the report cite?
2. What percentage of eighth graders drink alcohol, according to the authors?
3. What harms are associated with beginning to drink early in life, according to the report?

Alcohol use by children, adolescents, and young adults under the legal drinking age of 21 produces human tragedies with alarming regularity. Motor vehicle crashes, homicides, suicides, and other unintentional injuries are the four leading causes of death of 15- to 20-year-olds, and alcohol is a factor in many of these deaths. Indeed, so many underage drinkers die in car crashes that this problem, by itself, is a major national concern. In relation to the number of licensed drivers, young people under age 21 who have been drinking are involved in fatal crashes at twice the rate of adult drivers.

Car crashes are the most visible and most numbing consequences of underage drinking, but they represent only a small proportion of the social toll that underage drinking takes on the present and future welfare of society. Other damaging problems include dangerous sexual practices that lead to both serious disease and unwanted pregnancies, unintentional injuries, fights, and school failures that lead to expulsions or withdrawals. [D.T.] Levy et al. estimated that in 1996 underage drinking led to 3,500 deaths, 2 million nonfatal injuries, 1,200 cases of fetal alcohol syndrome, and 57,000 cases of treatment for alcohol dependence. Worse yet, underage drinking reaches into the future by impeding normal development and constricting future opportunities. Conservatively estimated, the social cost of underage drinking in the United States in 1996 was $52.8 billion.

Starting Early

For many children, alcohol use begins early, during a critical developmental period: in 2002, 19.6 percent of eighth graders were current users of alcohol (use within the past 30 days), which can be compared with 10.7 percent who smoked cigarettes and 8.3 percent who used marijuana. Among each older age cohort of high school students,

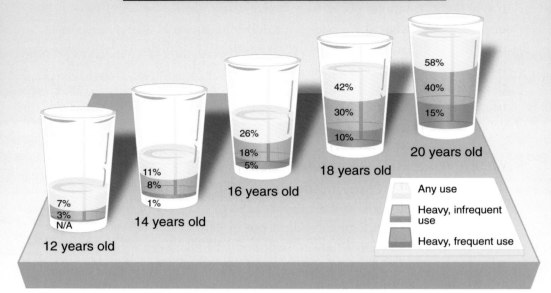

Percent of Young People Who Drink and Frequency of Use

12 years old
7%
3%
N/A

14 years old
11%
8%
1%

16 years old
26%
18%
5%

18 years old
42%
30%
10%

20 years old
58%
40%
15%

Any use

Heavy, infrequent use

Heavy, frequent use

Source: National Research Council and the Institute of Medicine, *Reducing Underage Drinking: A Collective Responsibility,* 2004.

the prevalence, frequency, and intensity of drinking increase, contributing to increasing rates of educational failure, injury, and death as children move from grade to grade. By the time young people are seniors in high school, almost three-quarters (71.5 percent) report having drunk in the past year, almost half (48.6 percent) are current drinkers, and more than one-quarter (28.6 percent) report having had five or more drinks in a row in the past 2 weeks. Among 18- to 22-year-olds, 41.4 percent of full-time college students and 35.9 percent of other young adults report heavy drinking. Heavy childhood and teenage drinking injures the developing brain and otherwise interferes with important developmental tasks. In addition, children and adolescents who begin drinking early are more likely than others to wind up with alcohol problems throughout their adult lives.

The public is certainly aware of these problems, especially drunk driving by teens. However, recent surveys demonstrate that parents underestimate the prevalence and intensity of alcohol use by their own children and by the underage population. Moreover, as measured by media attention and government expenditures, public concern about teenage alcohol use has not been remotely commensurate with the magnitude of the problem. A telling measure of the current societal response is the large gap in the federal government's investment in discouraging illicit drug use among teenagers and in discouraging underage drinking, given that the social damage from underage alcohol use far exceeds the harms caused by illicit drug use. In fiscal 2000, the nation spent approximately $1.8 billion on preventing illicit drug use, which was 25 times the amount, $71.1 million, targeted at preventing underage alcohol use. The amount spent on preventing underage drinking also appears to be less than the amount spent on preventing tobacco use: in fiscal 2000, the Office of Smoking and Health, only one of many agencies in the Department of Health and Human Services concerned with smoking prevention, spent approximately $100 million. In addition, the states spent a great deal more, including funds generated by the agreement that settled the states' Medicaid reimbursement suits against the tobacco companies.

Liquor store clerks across the country are fighting underage drinking by using a device like this one that can detect counterfeit identification cards.

Growing Awareness of the Problem

There are signs that public attention to underage drinking is increasing and that the public recognizes the need to address the problem more aggressively than has thus far occurred. A . . . [2002] study [by A.C. Wagenaar et al.] on public attitudes toward underage drinking shows almost universal recognition of this problem. In fact, 98 percent of adults polled said they were concerned about teen drinking and 66 percent said they were "very concerned." Moreover, a majority of respondents favored strong regulatory actions, such as additional controls on alcohol sales and advertising that would "make it harder for teenagers to get alcoholic beverages." In 1999, Mothers Against Drunk Driving (MADD) added the goal of reducing underage drinking to its

For these L.A. high school students, an empty casket decorated with flowers serves as a grim reminder of the danger associated with drunk driving.

mission statement, and its activities and public statements increasingly reflect this focus. Underage drinking has also won the attention of the spouses of the nation's governors, many of whom have come together to form the Leadership to Keep Children Alcohol Free, in collaboration with the Robert Wood Johnson Foundation (RWJF) and the National Institute on Alcohol Abuse and Alcoholism (NIAAA, part of the National Institutes of Health). In collaboration with the American Medical Association (AMA), the RWJF has also provided long-term support to 12 community and 10 university-based coalitions with the specific mission of reducing and preventing underage drinking. The AMA has itself also become increasingly active on the issue of underage drinking, calling for tighter regulation of alcohol availability, higher excise taxes, and restrictions on alcohol advertising. Members of the alcohol industry also have continued their efforts to discourage underage drinking through responsible drinking campaigns and approaches such as server, parent, and youth-oriented education and involvement in prevention efforts on college campuses.

> **FAST FACT**
>
> According to the National Center on Addiction and Substance Abuse at Columbia University, teenagers who drink heavily are more than twice as likely as nondrinkers to report deliberately trying to hurt themselves or kill themselves. They are also more than twice as likely to think about killing themselves.

Underage drinking has also begun to attract increased government attention in Washington. The U.S. Federal Trade Commission (FTC), at the request of Congress, recently reviewed the alcohol industry's advertising and marketing practices. Its [1999] report called on alcohol companies to move toward the "best practices" in the industry "to reduce underage alcohol ad exposure." In 2003 Congress called on the FTC to revisit its inquiry into alcohol advertising and youth and to investigate if and how the recommendations issued in its 1999 report have been implemented by the alcohol industry. Advocacy groups have also urged Congress to include underage alcohol use in the major media campaign being waged against illegal drug use under the auspices of the Office of National Drug Control Policy. . . .

Source: Gamble. © 2002 by *The Florida Times-Union.* Reproduced by permission.

Need for Consensus

An effective strategy to reduce a behavior as pervasive and widely facil-
itated as underage drinking will depend on a public consensus about
both goals and means, which will require an unequivocal commitment
from a broad array of public and private institutions. If the nation is
to succeed in promoting abstention or reduced consumption by minors
in a country that has more than 120 million drinkers, the need to do
so has to be understood and embraced by many people in a position
to reduce drinking opportunities for minors. An effective strategy will
depend on adoption of public policies by authoritative decision makers about how to use tax money and public authority—for example,
whether to use federal dollars to fund a national media campaign, how
to enforce existing state laws banning sales to underage drinkers, or
how local school boards should discipline students who drink. The
process of enacting such policies will require some degree of public
consensus, but this is only the start.

Ultimately, the effectiveness of government policies will depend on
how enthusiastically a great many public and private agencies join in
the effort to implement them. If parents, animated by a national media

campaign, join local police and school boards in concerted efforts to discourage underage drinking and if alcohol distributors join with regulatory agencies to find means to deny underage drinkers easy access to alcohol, then the impact of government policies will be increased. In short, a public consensus to deal determinedly and effectively with underage drinking is needed not only to generate support for adopting strong policies, but also to make them effective. Conversely, both enactment and implementation will be seriously impeded if the public is divided or ambivalent about the importance of reducing underage drinking.

EVALUATING THE AUTHORS' ARGUMENTS:

The viewpoint you just read lists many statistics on the harmful effects of underage drinking. Do you think teenagers who read this viewpoint will be persuaded to not drink? Explain your answer.

The Problem of Teen Alcohol Abuse Is Exaggerated

Nick Gillespie

"Alcohol consumption by teenagers dropped sharply."

In the following viewpoint Nick Gillespie argues that a prohibitionist attitude has led to a tendency to exaggerate the problem of teen alcohol abuse in America. Specifically, he responds to a report issued by an organization that seeks to reduce drug and alcohol abuse by young people. According to Gillespie, the report vastly overstates the amount of alcohol consumed by teenagers. When confronted with the true statistics on teen alcohol use, the organization's spokesperson refused to fully acknowledge the mistake. Moreover, the newspaper reporting the story resorted to a sensationalistic anecdote that served to reinforce the distorted view of teen alcohol abuse. Nick Gillespie is the editor in chief of *Reason,* a journal of opinion published by the Reason Institute, a libertarian think tank.

I n February [2002], Columbia University's Center on Addiction and Substance Abuse (CASA) released the policy wonk equivalent of a Girls Gone Wild spring break video. *Teen Tipplers: America's Underage Drinking Epidemic* promised a salacious expose of youth gone very, very bad. The most ballyhooed factoid in the widely covered report, available online at www.casacolumbia.org, certainly seemed to deliver the goods; CASA declared that zit-faced lushes between the ages of 12 and 20 consume a whopping 25 percent of all alcohol sold in this sweet land of libertines.

College students in Florida enjoy a sunny spring-break day. Some people argue that stories of excessive alcohol consumption during spring break are grossly exaggerated.

"Drinking is teen America's fatal attraction . . . a deadly round of Russian roulette," claimed CASA's head honcho, Joseph A. Califano Jr., in the casually apocalyptic and cliche-ridden phraseology favored by our public policy puritans. You only had to wonder how he restrained himself from denouncing teens and booze as the most terrifying twosome since Frankenstein met the Wolf Man.

There was just one problem with *Teen Tipplers'* headline-grabbing finding: It was about as legit as Jenna Bush's ID card. How CASA and its journalistic designated driver, *The New York Times,* handled the screw up reveals a lot about America's ongoing war between wets and drys. Although Prohibition was repealed almost 70 years ago, the prohibitionist mind-set was not. It's alive and well, and looking to turn any drop of liquor into a sign of pathology.

A Grudging Admission

The day after *Teen Tipplers* hit the news, CASA grudgingly admitted that the proper estimate for the underage share of alcohol consump-

Underage drinkers are responsible for 11.4 percent of alcohol consumption in the United States, a number much lower than anti-alcohol advocates allege.

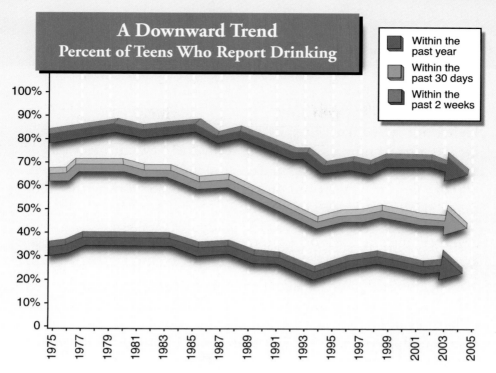

A Downward Trend
Percent of Teens Who Report Drinking

- ■ Within the past year
- ■ Within the past 30 days
- ■ Within the past 2 weeks

Source: National Research Council and the Institute of Medicine, *Reducing Underage Drinking: A Collective Responsibility*, 2004.

tion is 11.4 percent, not 25 percent. The group's mistake stemmed from a failure to adjust for oversampling of younger drinkers in the federal government's National Household Survey on Drug Abuse. Caught in an obvious and undeniable mathematical mistake, CASA argued like a late-night drunk that really, man, no, really, man, it was still absolutely right in its original conclusion.

"It's very unfortunate," CASA's vice president and director of policy research, Sue Foster, told the *Times*. "We didn't reweight the data. But we think the 11.4 percent number is way too low, since there's so much underreporting."

The *Times* headlined its February 27 story containing the above quote "Disturbing Finding on Young Drinkers Proves to Be Wrong." Did it ever. Reporter Tamar Lewin further noted that "alcohol consumption by teenagers dropped sharply in the 1980's, when states raised the drinking age to 21 from 18." There's more: "The proportion of teenagers who engage in binge drinking (i.e. consuming five or more drinks on a single occasion] has declined. . . . In 1998, 6.6 percent of girls and 8.7 percent of boys 12 to 17 reported binge drinking, compared with 11 percent of the girls and nearly 19 percent of the boys a decade earlier."

An Over-the-Top Ending

Here's the crazed part: Despite such sober trends, the *Times* piece quickly turned into a sermon. The really bad news, it turns out, is that the historical gender gap in teen drinking has all but disappeared, with 41 percent of girls and 40 percent of boys reporting that they drank alcohol in the previous month.

The last quarter of Lewin's article is about "Natalie, 17, a senior at a Brooklyn private school who attends Alcoholics Anonymous meetings." Natalie, we learn, was hitting the sauce like Betty Ford by age 14. She bottomed out "drinking gin out of a McDonald's coffee cup [as] a homeless man who had overdosed on heroin died right in front of her." And hey kids, in case you miss the moral of all this, Natalie declares, "I don't want to drink ever again; I know where drinking takes me, and it's not pretty."

It sure isn't. Neither is a "widely respected antidrinking organization" (the *Times*' description of CASA) that can't add or simply admit when it has wildly overstated its case. Or a paper of record that ends a story about the mistake with an over-the-top Gin Lane set piece about the evils of drink.

EVALUATING THE AUTHOR'S ARGUMENTS:

Identify two passages in Nick Gillespie's viewpoint in which the author uses humor. What point is he attempting to make by using humor in these passages? Does he succeed? Why or why not?

Teen Alcohol Use Can Be Beneficial

Rutger C.M.E. Engels

"Alcohol use may . . . increase feelings of self-esteem and decrease feelings of stress and loneliness among adolescents."

In the following viewpoint, Rutger C.M.E. Engels argues that moderate drinking can have positive consequences for teenagers. Because most older adolescents drink, he notes, those who do not drink are more likely to be socially ostracized and experience depression and low self-esteem. In addition, because drinking is normal behavior for adults, drinking helps teens make the transition from childhood to adulthood. Engels acknowledges that drinking can have negative consequences for some teens, especially those who drink heavily or who drink to avoid negative emotions. However, he concludes that teens who drink moderately are more likely to develop into happy and well-adjusted adults. Engels is a professor at the Institute of Family and Child Care Studies at the University of Nijmegen in the Netherlands.

AS YOU READ, CONSIDER THE FOLLOWING QUESTIONS:
1. What are the five functions of drinking for adolescents, as outlined by Engels?
2. How does being in alcohol-related settings reduce stress among adolescents, according to the author?

National surveys in Western societies, such as the United States, Great Britain, and the Netherlands have shown that experimentation with potentially risky behaviors, such as cigarette smoking, marijuana use, and alcohol consumption, is usual among adolescents. For example, in these studies, only 10% to 15% of late adolescents reported abstaining from alcohol. Indeed, nonexperimentation, particularly in the older age categories, might be considered statistically deviant. The widespread uptake of alcohol in adolescence focuses attention on the tasks to be realized in the teenage years. One of the most prominent issues in the teenage years concerns the development and maintenance of friendships and romantic relationships. In particular, adolescents seek company with their peers in specific situations outside the parental home. Many leisure-time activities of adolescents take place in alcohol-related settings, such as bars, night clubs, and parties. Furthermore, a part of the normal maturation process consists of adopting adult-like attitudes and behaviors. Because most adults consume alcohol, it is not surprising that young people adopt this habit. . . .

In this article, I examine the functions of drinking for adolescents more closely and discuss a framework of the facilitating functions of drinking by highlighting studies on these issues. Drinking has several functions. First, drinking is related to several characteristics of the intensity and quality of friendships. Second, adolescent alcohol use is related to dating and involvement in romantic relationships. Third, drinking is associated with psychologic developmental tasks in adolescence, such as enhancement of autonomy and formation of identity. Fourth, adolescent alcohol use is associated with the separation process from parents. Fifth, alcohol use may, through its social features, increase feelings of self-esteem and decrease feelings of stress and loneliness among adolescents. Finally, drinking may involve discovering some of the boundaries in life, exemplified by risky behaviors, such as minor delinquent acts, smoking, drinking and use of "soft" drugs. . . .

> **FAST FACT**
>
> According to *Education Health* magazine, teens cite various reasons for drinking alcohol, including the following:
>
> • To overcome shyness
> • To escape loneliness
> • To relax and loosen up
> • To be part of a group

Alcohol is often an integral part of social events such as dances and parties.

Alcohol Improves Friendships

The transition from adolescence to adulthood is accompanied by intensified contacts with peers and an entrance into new social contexts and activities. The concerns that adolescents have to achieve intimacy goals, such as closeness and trust, are redirected from parents toward peers. It is essential for them to come in contact with new friends or strengthen existing bonds. In this way adolescents can reflect their own ideas, opinions, and emotional development. When youngsters are asked what motives they have for drinking, they often mention the social aspects of drinking. Adolescents believe drinking makes parties more fun, it makes one more relaxed, and it makes it easier to approach others and to share feelings and experiences. . . . There is substantial support for the assumption that young people who drink alcohol are more sociable, more integrated in their peer group, have better peer relations, and experience fewer feelings of loneliness. . . .

Alcohol and the Maturing Process

The adolescent years are characterized by an increasing attention to adult-like behaviors and opinions. By looking at how adults act and

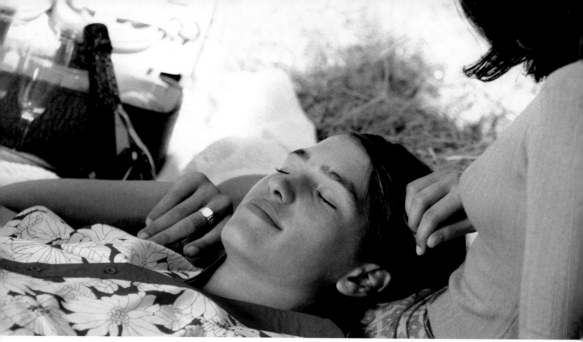

A young couple relaxes together with a bottle of champagne. Patterns of alcohol consumption among teens typically mirror those of adults.

how they are portrayed in the media, teenagers learn about the norms and values of adults. Because drinking is rather normative behavior among adults in most Western societies, youngsters adopt it. In other words, starting to drink is one of the ways they orientate to the adult world. Drinking is not a unique characteristic connected to youth cultures but is a reflection of societal norms and values. In addition, drinking creates an opportunity for adolescents to undertake activities without their parents, and drinking also distinguishes them from the younger generation. Drinking may also be related to other transition behaviors, such as financial independence through a job, an interest in future positions in society, dating, mating, and leaving the parental home.

Other psychologic changes in adolescent lives involve gaining autonomy, forming identity, and getting a clear self-definition. Coming out from under the wings of their parents makes adolescents more independent and mature. In particular, more intensive contacts with friends and partners lead to enhanced feelings of autonomy and the impression that they are able to handle things on their own. Having a job and creating opportunities to fulfill emotional and social needs outside the parental home results in feelings of autonomy. Attendance in alcohol-related settings builds opportunities to fulfill the needs for independence. Regarding identity formation, [R.M.] Jones and [B.R.] Hartman showed that average drinking levels in adolescents are related to a more mature and sophisticated identity stature. Youngsters with low and high consumption levels were more likely to have a "diffused" identity.

Psychological Well-Being

Drinking and pub going by adolescents can be seen as a collectively appreciated time-out situation in which it is legitimate to forget the everyday obligations. Furthermore, it facilitates the sharing of activities, experiences, and emotions with peers. The exchange of common experiences and the knowledge that others are in a similar position positively affects youngsters' well-being. For instance, engagement in social activities with friends is associated with healthier emotional functioning. It follows that if the potential advantages of entrance in alcohol-related settings for this age group are considered, not entering these types of settings might be related to loneliness, isolation, and stress. Perhaps people who do not drink on a regular basis have fewer opportunities to relieve their daily stress or to associate with peers. This point of view is related to the ideas of [H.] Pape and [T.] Hammer on alcohol abstinence in late adolescence

Research has shown that teen alcohol use often accompanies other coming-of-age behaviors such as dating.

and young adulthood. They emphasize that alcohol use is the norm for people in this period of life. Deviating from the mainstream is associated with negative aspects, such as a lack of social integration as well as low self-esteem and feelings of depression.

Testing the Limits

[J.] Shedler and [J.] Block found that young Americans who are not curious and open for new experiences are more likely to refrain from substance use in the adolescent years. Because it is atypical and nonnormative for youngsters to remain abstainers, this nondrinking could be perceived as indicative of fear of losing control, being timid, and suffering from a lack of "normal" sensation seeking. Some indirect support for this assumption has been found. It is widely known that certain forms of substance use and delinquent behaviors co-occur. For example, those who abstain from drinking are also less likely to smoke, to experiment with marijuana, to commit minor criminal acts, and to be truants or rebels at school. Thus, in some individuals, abstinence is a sign of a relatively sober and conservative lifestyle without many risk-taking behaviors.

This does not imply that we should ignore adolescent drinking or that we should stimulate youngsters to drink alcohol. First and foremost, our concern should be directed to identify adolescents who do not drink for social reasons but who drink to forget feelings of stress and depression or a lack of self-esteem; who drink heavily and irresponsibly, with accompanying adverse results such as aggression, violent acts, sexual harassment, or drunk driving; or to help those who continue their high levels throughout young adulthood and become problem drinkers. Parents and policy makers should worry less about the majority of adolescents who drink moderately and more about adolescents who do not.

EVALUATING THE AUTHOR'S ARGUMENTS:

In the viewpoint you just read, Rutger C.M.E. Engels lists several reasons why he believes alcohol use among adolescents can be beneficial. Do you find his arguments persuasive? Why or why not?

Alcohol Abuse Among College Students Is a Crisis

National Institute on Alcohol Abuse and Alcoholism

"The consequences of excessive college drinking are more widespread and destructive than most people realize."

The National Institute on Alcohol Abuse and Alcoholism (NIAAA), a part of the National Institutes of Health, is a department of the federal government whose mission is to address alcohol-related problems in society. In 2002, the NIAAA issued a report called *A Call to Action: Changing the Culture of Drinking at U.S. Colleges,* from which the following viewpoint was excerpted. The NIAAA reports that drinking among college students is rampant. Especially alarming, according to the report, is the large number of college students who binge drink, which is defined for men as drinking five drinks in a row and for women as drinking four drinks in a row. The high rate of drinking among college students has catastrophic consequences, according to the NIAAA, often causing death, sexual abuse, and poor academic performance.

National Institute on Alcohol Abuse and Alcoholism, *A Call to Action: Changing the Culture of Drinking at U.S. Colleges,* Bethesda, MD, April 2002.

AS YOU READ, CONSIDER THE FOLLOWING QUESTIONS:
1. What aspects of the college environment encourage student drinking, according to the NIAAA?
2. How many college students die each year from alcohol-related accidents, as reported by the NIAAA?
3. What percentage of college students report that they binge drink, according to the authors?

O ther than the damage and injuries that occur during spring break each year, the only consequences of college drinking that usually come to the public's attention are occasional student deaths from alcohol overuse (e.g., alcohol poisoning) or other alcohol-related tragedies. They prompt a brief flurry of media attention; then, the topic disappears until the next incident. In fact, the consequences of college drinking are much more than occasional; at least 1,400 college student deaths a year are linked to alcohol. . . . High-risk drinking also results in serious injuries, assaults, and other health and academic problems, and is a major factor in damage to institutional property. The relative scarcity of headlines about college drinking belies an important fact: the consequences of excessive college drinking are more widespread and destructive than most people realize. While only isolated incidents tend to make news, many school presidents conclude that these pervasive, albeit less obvious, problems are occurring on their campuses at the same time. . . .

College Drinking Is a Culture

The tradition of drinking has developed into a kind of culture—beliefs and customs—entrenched in every level of college students' environments. Customs handed down through generations of college drinkers reinforce students' expectation that alcohol is a necessary ingredient for social success. These beliefs and the expectations they engender exert a powerful influence over students' behavior toward alcohol.

Customs that promote college drinking also are embedded in numerous levels of students' environments. The walls of college sports arenas carry advertisements from alcohol industry sponsors. Alumni carry on the alcohol tradition, perhaps less flamboyantly than during their college years, at sports events and alumni social functions. Communities permit establishments near campus to serve or sell alcohol, and these establishments depend on the college clientele for their financial success.

Students derive their expectations of alcohol from their environment and from each other, as they face the insecurity of establishing themselves in a new social milieu. Environmental and peer influences combine to create a culture of drinking. This culture actively promotes drinking, or passively promotes it, through tolerance, or even tacit approval, of college drinking as a rite of passage. . . .

The Consequences of College Drinking

The consequences of excessive and underage drinking affect virtually all college campuses, college communities, and college students, whether they choose to drink or not.

Death: 1,400 college students between the ages of 18 and 24 die each year from alcohol-related unintentional injuries, including motor vehicle crashes.

Injury: 500,000 students between the ages of 18 and 24 are unintentionally injured under the influence of alcohol.

Assault: More than 600,000 students between the ages of 18 and 24 are assaulted by another student who has been drinking.

"... AND AS YOU SEE,—OUR CAMPUS IS ABSOLUTELY DRIPPING WITH TRADITION."

Sexual Abuse: More than 70,000 students between the ages of 18 and 24 are victims of alcohol-related sexual assault or date rape.

Unsafe Sex: 400,000 students between the ages of 18 and 24 had unprotected sex and more than 100,000 students between the ages of 18 and 24 report having been too intoxicated to know if they consented to having sex.

Academic Problems: About 25 percent of college students report academic consequences of their drinking including missing class, falling behind, doing poorly on exams or papers, and receiving lower grades overall.

Health Problems/Suicide Attempts: More than 150,000 students develop an alcohol-related health problem, and between 1.2 and 1.5 percent of students indicate that they tried to commit suicide within the past year due to drinking or drug use.

Drunk Driving: 2.1 million students between the ages of 18 and 24 drove under the influence of alcohol last year [2001].

Vandalism: About 11 percent of college student drinkers report that they have damaged property while under the influence of alcohol.

Property Damage: More than 25 percent of administrators from schools with relatively low drinking levels and over 50 percent from schools with high drinking levels say their campuses have a "moderate" or "major" problem with alcohol-related property damage.

Police Involvement: About 5 percent of 4-year college students are involved with the police or campus security as a result of their drinking, and an estimated 110,000 students between the ages of 18 and 24 are arrested for an alcohol-related violation such as public drunkenness or driving under the influence.

Alcohol Abuse and Dependence: 31 percent of college students met criteria for a diagnosis of alcohol abuse and 6 percent for a diagnosis of alcohol dependence in the past 12 months, according to questionnaire-based self-reports about their drinking.

A woman at a Washington, D.C., press conference sits next to a portrait of her son, a college student who died after binge drinking.

Binge Drinking

Data from several national surveys indicate that about four in five college students drink and that about half of college student drinkers engage in heavy episodic consumption. Recent concerns have, therefore, often focused on the practice of binge drinking, typically defined as consuming five or more drinks in a row for men, and four or more drinks in a row for women. A shorthand description of this type of heavy episodic drinking is the "5/4 definition." Approximately two of five college students—more than 40 percent—have engaged in binge drinking at least once during the past 2 weeks, according to this definition. It should be noted, however, that colleges vary widely in their binge drinking rates—from 1 percent to more than 70 percent—and a study on one campus may not apply to others.

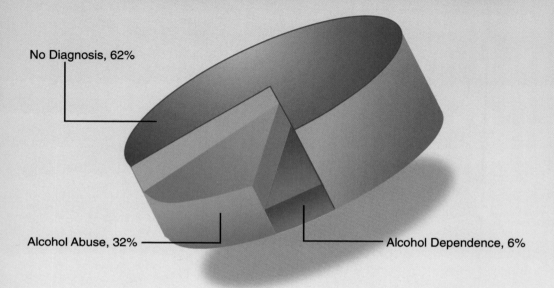

Percent of College Students Diagnosed with Alcohol Abuse or Dependence

No Diagnosis, 62%

Alcohol Abuse, 32%

Alcohol Dependence, 6%

Source: From data from J.R. Knight et al., "Alcohol Abuse and Dependence Among U.S. College Students," *Journal of Studies on Alcohol,* May 2002.

The U.S. Surgeon General and the U.S. Department of Health and Human Services (USDHHS) have identified binge drinking among college students as a major public health problem. In "Healthy People 2010," which sets U.S. public health goals through the year 2010, the Federal government has singled out binge drinking among college students for a specific, targeted reduction (e.g., from 39 percent to 20 percent) by the year 2010. "Healthy People 2010" notes that: "Binge drinking is a national problem, especially among males and young adults." The report also observes that: "The perception that alcohol use is socially acceptable correlates with the fact that more than 80 percent of American youth consume alcohol before their 21st birthday, whereas the lack of social acceptance of other drugs correlates with comparatively lower rates of use. Similarly, widespread societal expectations that young persons will engage in binge drinking may encourage this highly dangerous form of alcohol consumption."

There is evidence that more extreme forms of drinking by college students are escalating. In one study, frequent binge drinkers (defined as three times or more in the past 2 weeks) grew from 20 percent to 23 percent between 1993 and 1999. The number of students who reported three or more incidents of intoxication in the past month also increased. It should be noted, however, that the number of college students who do not drink is also growing. In the same study, the percentage of abstainers increased from 15 to 19 percent.

EVALUATING THE AUTHORS' ARGUMENTS:

The viewpoint you just read was written by a government agency whose purpose is to address social problems related to alcohol. The next viewpoint was written by a scholar with the Cato Institute. This organization is a think tank that adheres to the political philosophy of libertarianism, which opposes government involvement in citizens' personal decisions. Does knowing the source of these two viewpoints influence your reading of them? How so?

The Problem of Alcohol Abuse Among College Students Is Overstated

Steven Milloy

"There aren't statistically meaningful differences in rates of alcohol-related problems between college students and non–college students."

In the following viewpoint, Steven Milloy argues that drinking among college students has been exaggerated. He focuses specifically on a 2002 report published by the National Institute on Alcohol Abuse and Alcoholism (NIAAA) stating that college drinking is a widespread problem that results in numerous deaths, injuries, assaults, and other problems. Milloy contends that the conclusions reached in the NIAAA report are based on flawed research methods. Drinking among college students is no more serious than drinking among noncollege youths, he concludes. Steven Milloy is a scholar at the Cato Institute, a libertarian think tank. He is also the author of *Junk Science Judo: Self-Defense Against Health Scares and Scams.*

AS YOU READ, CONSIDER THE FOLLOWING QUESTIONS:
1. How did researcher Ralph Hingson arrive at the number of 1,445 alcohol-related deaths a year, according to Milloy? And why is this method inaccurate?
2. How does the National Highway Traffic Safety Administration define a fatal crash as being alcohol related, as stated by Milloy? Why does this method lead to an inflated statistic, in his opinion?
3. What is the goal of Mothers Against Drunk Driving, according to the author?

This week's news about excessive college drinking is another shocking example of statistical deception by shameless activists manipulating a media panting for sensationalism.

USA Today's "College drinking kills 1,400 a year, study finds" was the typical headline.

The frenzy was sparked by the National Institute on Alcohol Abuse and Alcoholism's report, "A Call to Action: Changing the Culture of Drinking at U.S. Colleges."

In addition to the alleged death toll, the report's other alarmist claims include: 500,000 college students are injured while under the influence of alcohol; 600,000 are assaulted; 70,000 are the victims of sexual assault; 400,000 had unsafe sex; 25 percent have academic problems; and 150,000 have alcohol-related health problems or tried to commit suicide.

Statistical Guesswork

If true, these figures would make college worthy of a surgeon general's warning.

But none of these likely-to-be-immortalized factoids resulted from an actual count. They've been produced by statistical guesswork.

"A Call to Action" doesn't present the analysis behind these claims. It only references a new study simultaneously published in the *Journal of Studies on Alcohol* (March 2002). The study's lead author is Ralph Hingson of the Boston University School of Public Health.

As an example of how goofy Mr. Hingson's numbers are, here's how he calculated the headline-grabbing estimate of 1,400 deaths.

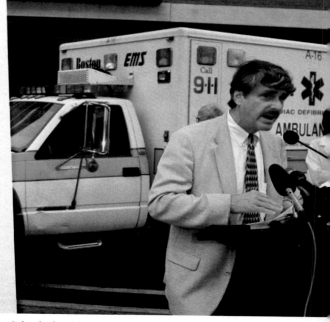

If all motorists in Massachusetts wore Safety Belts there would be

- 75-100 fewer traffic deaths each year; and
- 15,000 fewer injuries.

Ralph Hingson of the Boston University School of Public Health, seen here promoting the use of seat belts, asserts that drinking claims the lives of 1,400 college students every year.

There are about 25.5 million 18- to 24-year-olds living in the U.S., according to U.S. Census data. Thirty-one percent of this age group are enrolled as full- or part-time students in two- or four-year colleges.

The number of alcohol-related motor vehicle crash deaths among 18–24 year olds during 1998 is 3,674. Thirty-one percent of this figure is 1,138.

Similarly applying the 31 percent factor to the 991 alcohol-related, nontraffic deaths among 18- to 24-year-olds in 1998 results in an additional 307 deaths.

Adding the 307 and 1,138 figures equals the alleged 1,445 alcohol-related deaths annually among college students.

But Mr. Hingson relies on a key, but unsupported assumption. It does not automatically follow that college students constitute 31 percent of alcohol deaths simply because 31 percent of 18- to 24-year-olds are college students.

The simplistic reasoning is equivalent to assuming that because women constitute about half the population, they commit half of all crime. In fact, men commit more than 75 percent of crime.

An Inaccurate Definition of "Alcohol-Related"

The definition of what constitutes an "alcohol-related" death is another problem.

The National Highway Traffic Safety Administration defines a fatal traffic crash as being alcohol-related if either a driver or a pedestrian had a blood alcohol concentration (BAC) of 0.01 grams per deciliter (g/dl).

But 0.10 g/dl is the traditional level at which persons are considered to be intoxicated. Just because a person involved in a fatal accident has a measurable BAC doesn't mean the alcohol caused or contributed to the accident.

A police officer administers a Breathalyzer test to a suspected drunk driver. This test measures the driver's blood alcohol level.

Since 1980 Mothers Against Drunk Driving (MADD) has worked zealously to reduce the number of drunk-driving fatalities.

Even accepting Mr. Hingson's results at face value, his study is still silly.

There aren't statistically meaningful differences in rates of alcohol-related problems between college students and non–college students.

Mr. Hingson estimates, for example, that 41 percent of college students binge on occasion as compared to 36.5 percent of non–college students. But the relative difference between the two estimates (14 percent) is too small to be reliably detected by his crude data and analysis.

Also, if college students have alcohol problems in proportion to their presence in the age group, why crack down only on college students? Are the other 69 percent of 18- to 24-year-olds not worthy of attention?

A Crusade Against All Drinking

Why is Mr. Hingson playing fast and loose with the data?

He's on the board of directors of Mothers Against Drunk Driving (MADD).

Although MADD began in 1980 with the laudable goal of reducing drunk-driving fatalities, it has strayed beyond its original mission. "If truth-in-advertising laws applied to Mothers Against Drunk Driving, its name would be changed to Mothers Against All Drinking of Any Kind," says the Center for Consumer Freedom.

MADD's crusade has turned into a prohibitionist movement. Focusing on college kids and pressuring universities seems to be the new tactic to implement its misguided goal.

Mark Goldman, co-chair of the NIAAA task force that produced "A Call to Action" told the *Los Angeles Times,* "Our society has always dealt with [college drinking] with a wink and a nod, as a rite of passage. But the statistics that Ralph Hingson has put together are stunning to all of us, even the most seasoned researchers."

This scam must be very intoxicating. How can "seasoned researchers" fall for such obviously flawed analysis? Will they also be using the movie *Animal House* as evidence of excessive college drinking?

There is no question that some alcohol abuse occurs among college students—as it does among all 18- to 24-year-olds. However, this is hardly news or an excuse for junk science.

EVALUATING THE AUTHORS' ARGUMENTS:

The viewpoint in this chapter by the National Institute on Alcohol Abuse and Alcoholism cites numerous statistics to support its claim that drinking among college students is a serious problem. The viewpoint by Steven Milloy criticizes the methods used to arrive at these statistics. Does Milloy's analysis alter your faith in the accuracy of the NIAAA viewpoint? Why or why not? After reading both viewpoints, do you believe the problem of alcohol abuse by college students is particularly serious? Explain your answer.

CHAPTER 2

How Can Underage Drinking Be Prevented?

A plainclothes police officer confronts an underage drinker caught buying a bottle of alcohol in a supermarket.

VIEWPOINT 1

Raising Alcohol Taxes Can Prevent Underage Drinking

Jim Gogek

"Several studies show higher taxes particularly cut drinking by teenagers."

In 2003 a report commissioned by Congress listed raising alcohol taxes among its various recommendations for preventing underage drinking. In the following viewpoint, Jim Gogek argues that raising alcohol taxes is an effective way to keep teens from drinking. In addition, he contends that such taxes have not kept pace with inflation and do not sufficiently cover the costs of alcohol-related problems. Raising taxes can help hold the alcohol industry responsible for the problems its products cause to young people, he concludes. Jim Gogek is an editorial writer for the *San Diego Union-Tribune* newspaper.

AS YOU READ, CONSIDER THE FOLLOWING QUESTIONS:
1. What are the economic costs of alcohol abuse, as reported by Gogek? And how do they compare to alcohol tax revenues?
2. Why do higher taxes reduce drinking by teens, according to the author?
3. What percentage of alcohol does Gogek say is purchased by underage drinkers?

In the next few months [April–June 2003], legislators across the country, struggling with the worst fiscal crisis to hit states since World War II, will cut the financing of social programs. This will probably mean the demise of many alcohol and drug programs that keep adults out of jails and emergency rooms and children out of foster care and juvenile halls.

There is a solution: raise alcohol taxes to pay for social services. Taxes on alcohol don't even begin to pay the costs of alcohol abuse. Federal estimates put those costs at $185 billion, while federal, state and local alcohol tax revenues total about $18 billion.

Alcohol excise taxes used to be a significant slice of federal budget receipts, representing 11 percent in 1941. Today, they're less than 1 percent and dropping. Because of pressure from the alcohol industry, federal liquor taxes have increased only twice since 1951, and beer and wine taxes only once. Meanwhile, a few states have raised taxes a little while others have cut them. With inflation, the real value of state alcohol taxes has fallen by half since 1966.

Reducing Alcohol Abuse

Increasing state alcohol taxes would not only provide more money to reduce problems caused by alcohol abuse, it would also reduce alcohol abuse itself by raising prices, according to a federal report to Congress.

Many people believe that increasing state taxes on alcohol would help to reduce the incidence of alcohol abuse.

A store clerk checks the ID of a young man buying alcohol. Some argue that raising alcohol taxes would help discourage teens from purchasing alcoholic beverages.

Several studies show higher taxes particularly cut drinking by teenagers, who have less money than adults to buy alcohol.

But probably the most compelling argument for raising alcohol taxes is this: it makes the industry shoulder a more equitable share of responsibility for the problems caused by alcohol abuse. And the fact is that the industry makes most of its profits from that abuse. Binge drinking (five or more drinks at a time) accounts for 83 percent of all alcohol consumed. And sales to under-age drinkers amount to nearly 20 percent of the total market, or about $20 billion in illegally purchased alcohol, according to a study . . . in *The Journal of the American Medical Association.*

> ## FAST FACT
>
> A report by the National Academy of Sciences states that 60 percent of eighth graders say alcohol is "fairly easy" or "very easy" to obtain. Ninety percent of twelfth graders say it is "fairly easy" or "very easy" to obtain.

Former California governor Gray Davis opted not to raise taxes on alcohol in his state.

Raising taxes would also make the heaviest drinkers pay more, which is fair because they're the ones associated with the worst alcohol-related problems.

It's worth noting that the alcohol lobby is more powerful than ever, and that it is a significant contributor to political campaigns. Beer wholesalers gave about $160,000 last year [2002] to politicians in New York. Gov. George Pataki is pushing a plan to cut beer taxes, despite a $12 billion shortfall over the next two years. The reduction would leave New York with some of the lowest beer taxes in the nation.

In California, the alcohol industry donated $2.4 million in 2002, including nearly $260,000 to Gov. Gray Davis. Mr. Davis has supported raising cigarette taxes to help close the state's $35 billion gap, but not alcohol taxes.

So far this year [2003], 17 states have proposed raising alcohol taxes, but many have retreated in the face of the uproar from the alcohol industry. Tax increase proposals are fading in Ohio, Georgia and New Mexico. The Maryland governor has promised to veto proposed sin taxes. In South Dakota, lobbyists for alcohol retailers and wholesalers just persuaded legislators to kill a bill that would have raised taxes a mere 4 cents per drink. Industry influence is paying off.

EVALUATING THE AUTHORS' ARGUMENTS:

In the viewpoint you just read, Jim Gogek argues that raising taxes will reduce teen drinking. In the next viewpoint, David K. Rehr contends that because most teens get their alcohol from adults rather than purchasing it directly, raising taxes will not work. Is this argument convincing? Why or why not? Do you think raising taxes will deter teens from drinking? Explain your answer.

Raising Alcohol Taxes Will Not Prevent Underage Drinking

David K. Rehr

"There is no reliable data indicating a pattern that higher taxes reduce illegal underage drinking."

David K. Rehr is the president of the National Beer Wholesalers Association, a trade organization that represents over twenty-two hundred beer companies. In the following viewpoint, he criticizes a report that was commissioned by Congress to study the problem of underage drinking and propose solutions. Most specifically, he opposes the report's recommendation to raise alcohol taxes. He insists that raising taxes will do nothing to prevent underage drinking but will punish adults who buy alcohol legally and drink responsibly. As an alternative to higher taxes, Rehr advocates programs that educate parents, teachers, and young people about the dangers of underage drinking.

AS YOU READ, CONSIDER THE FOLLOWING QUESTIONS:
 1. How much money does the government spend each year on efforts to prevent underage drinking, as reported by Rehr?

2. In what way did the National Academy of Sciences ignore the intent of Congress, according to the author?
3. What percentage of teens cite their parents as the primary influence over their decision whether to drink, according to the statistics provided by Rehr?

We all suffer when junk science falls into the hands of the few antialcohol activists in Congress and government bureaucrats who utilize unreliable data to drive their personal agendas. This unfortunately is the case with the recent National Academy of Sciences' (NAS) Institute of Medicine study on underage drinking.

Thankfully in this case those bureaucrats are in the minority and the overwhelming majority of Congress is committed to focusing on real solutions, not scare tactics, to fight the serious issue of illegal drinking among our nation's youth.

There is no question that until everyone under the age of 21 stops drinking illegally we can all do more. But the question taxpayers should be asking is, "Are the government's efforts to prevent illegal underage drinking working and, if not, should we continue to throw good money after bad?"

Most taxpayers probably are unaware that a 2001 Government Accounting Office (GAO) report revealed that 23 government agencies are spending at least 71.1 million tax dollars annually on efforts to prevent underage drinking, and approximately $769 million of grant money is allocated to the states to address prevention efforts.

> **FAST FACT**
>
> In a survey of Minnesota twelfth graders, 38 percent of those who reported drinking said they drank in their own home. Eighty-three percent said they drank in someone else's home.

The troubling part is that the report concluded the federal government doesn't know where that money is going or whether it is being spent effectively. In a time of budget deficits and a soft economy, the government can't afford to be so reckless with our tax dollars.

In 2002, $500,000 was allocated to the National Academy of Sciences for the study of underage drinking at a session of Congress, like the one shown here.

Ignoring the Intent of Congress

Last year [2002], when a few members of Congress were urging appropriators to fund a multimillion-dollar media campaign to fight underage drinking, Congress made the sound decision to exercise some oversight. What was needed, and what Congress requested, was a thorough review of which government and private-sector programs work and which do not.

The National Beer Wholesalers Association (NBWA) supported Congress and strongly advocated for a study to review all existing programs and identify those that work. Unfortunately, however, the NAS wasted that opportunity and the $500,000 in taxpayer money that was allocated for the audit by ignoring the intent of Congress.

Rather than focusing on existing programs that have been successful in fighting illegal underage drinking, the NAS panel blamed the products, the advertising, popular culture and the alcohol industry. After

more than one year and $500,000 spent, the panel recommended exact-
ly what a similar panel recommended 22 years ago: raising taxes on
adult consumers of legal drinking age.

Now the few members of Congress who align themselves with the neo-
Prohibitionist movement are trumpeting this study as a critical reason to
allocate millions of tax dollars for more government programs. The problem is this study never accomplished what Congress intended—an audit
of which programs are effective.

Some of the most effective programs are being conducted in our communities, not necessarily by government agencies. Private-sector groups,
foundations, nonprofit organizations and faith-based groups are avoid-
ing bureaucratic red tape and taking their message directly to homes
and schools. Congress needs to know what works.

It is beyond irresponsible that the NAS chose to disregard the instruc-
tions from Congress. When Congress asked for a comprehensive review

*Emotional students participate in a privately sponsored education program about drunk
driving. Many people applaud the efforts of private organizations to curb alcohol abuse.*

of existing programs, a reasonable assumption might have been to utilize existing research to build on the GAO report. This might have included an audit of federal-government programs and certainly would have sought input from those agencies that regulate licensed beverages, most importantly the state alcohol-beverage commissions.

Instead of focusing on existing programs implemented by federal, state and local governments, the alcohol industry, advocacy groups and others, the NAS chose to focus on raising taxes as a means to curb underage drinking. But this theory is not based on real science and falls flat when one reviews actual data.

Higher Taxes Do Not Work

For example, if higher taxes actually deter illegal underage drinking, then the rate of underage drinking should be well below average in states with the highest alcohol excise taxes such as Alaska, Florida, Hawaii and New York but that is not the case. While alcohol excise tax rates vary widely in the individual states, there is no reliable data indicating a pattern that higher taxes reduce illegal underage drinking.

Also, by the NAS report's own admission, the majority of underage drinkers obtain alcohol from adults. If this is true, and underage drinkers are helping themselves to the family liquor cabinet and refrigerator, then how will raising the price through taxes serve as a deterrent?

The simple fact is raising taxes will not curb illegal underage drinking, but it certainly will punish the more than 90 million adults of legal drinking age, mostly hardworking people of modest means who enjoy our products.

Focusing on Real Solutions

According to the 2003 Roper Youth Report, 73 percent of adolescents cite their parents, not cost or advertising, as the primary influence in their decisions about whether they drink alcohol. That is why the beer industry has focused on educating parents, teachers, community leaders and youth on the dangers of underage drinking.

Brewers and wholesalers in the United States have a long-standing commitment to initiatives to fight illegal underage drinking as well as programs to combat alcohol abuse and drunk driving, committing hundreds of millions of dollars toward successful efforts.

Young people willing to talk openly about alcohol with the adults in their lives are less likely to experiment with drinking.

Our industry-sponsored programs focus on real solutions, such as educational speakers in schools who encourage youth to stand up to peer pressure, materials to help parents talk to their children about not drinking, resources for law enforcement and retailers, and alcohol-free after-prom events. These efforts are working. In fact, 83 percent of the nation's youth are making the right decision to not drink alcohol illegally, according to government data.

Real progress is being made in the fight against illegal underage drinking. Of course more can be done and, working together, we can continue to make progress by focusing on real solutions. But raising taxes is not the answer. Neither is spending millions of taxpayer dollars on new and untested initiatives that have not proved to be successful. Unfortunately, the NAS panel results are not surprising considering that many of those chosen to serve as panelists came to the table with preconceived biases and ignored good scientific methods. . . .

Committed to the Fight

Notwithstanding these misguided efforts, the beer industry remains committed to the fight against illegal underage drinking. Let's focus on real solutions, such as the programs that are working in our communities, and not tax hikes and untested programs. Working together, we can keep alcohol out of the hands of our children.

> **EVALUATING THE AUTHOR'S ARGUMENTS:**
>
> The viewpoint you just read was written by the president of an organization that lobbies on behalf of the beer industry. Does knowing the author's background affect your reading of his article? Do you find his arguments more persuasive or less persuasive in light of this knowledge? Please explain.

Parents Can Help Prevent Underage Drinking

Barbara F. Meltz

"Parents can have extraordinary influence."

In the following viewpoint, Barbara F. Meltz argues that parents can have a significant impact on their teenage children's decisions about drinking. She insists that while teens may say they do not want their parents' advice and involvement, they will respond to parental influence if it is consistent and sincere. She contends that parents must convey information about the harms of alcohol, vigilantly observe their teens' behavior, and set clear rules against drinking. Meltz is a staff writer for the *Boston Globe* newspaper.

AS YOU READ, CONSIDER THE FOLLOWING QUESTIONS:
1. What reasons does Meltz list to explain why teens drink?
2. What are the three points about alcohol that parents need to convey to their children, according to the author?
3. What clues should parents look for when their children come home at night, according to Meltz?

Recently released studies highlight the problem of binge drinking among college students, but binging isn't unique to them. It's also a problem with high school students, including those as young as eighth grade. Researchers say parents tend not to realize how big a problem it is.

If the typical adult drinks to be social, the typical teenager drinks to get drunk.

"Binge is part of the social milieu on weekends for American adolescents. It's how partying is defined," says John Kulig, director of adolescent medicine at New England Medical Center.

The University of Michigan's "Monitoring the Future" 2001 nationwide survey reports that 13 percent of eighth-graders, 25 percent of 10th-graders, and 30 percent of 12th-graders said they had had five or more drinks in one sitting in the two weeks prior to the survey. Actual consumption could be more.

Binging is so popular that Stephen Wallace, national chairman of SADD (Students Against Destructive Decisions and Students Against Drunk Driving), says, "Parents should know that any kid today who drinks is at risk for binging." . . .

Why Teens Drink

There are several reasons why teenagers say they start drinking: boredom, curiosity, a wish to be more grown up, because their parents do. What young drinkers all have in common, however, is available liquor, usually from an older teenager or a parent's cabinet; a lack of supervision, especially when both parents work; and a friend who's game.

It's not that peers actively lobby each other to drink. Rather, teenagers tend to assume the behavior of their own peers is what's normal, so the pressure they feel is internal. Wallace says, "A lot of kids who binge look around to see what others are doing. Drinking games. Multiple shots of sweet-flavored drinks. Beer. Just because it's beer doesn't mean it isn't a problem. Not when you have five or more."

FAST FACT

According to the National Institutes of Health, children who begin drinking before the age of fifteen are four times as likely to become alcoholics as teens who abstain from drinking.

Recent studies suggest that a significant percentage of high school students have indulged in episodes of binge drinking.

Parents Have Influence

There is good news in the midst of all this. Although parents have less influence over a teenager than, say, over a 10-year-old, we have more influence than we realize. To exert it, though, we need to overcome the reality gap.

"There's a disconnect between the real world kids live in and the world parents think their kids live in," says Wallace. He tells of one study repeated around the country where teenagers were interviewed in one room and their parents in another. Over and over, he says, "You'd have a kid saying he drinks every night, every weekend, and his mother across the hall saying, 'I'm lucky my son doesn't drink.'"

In fact, the typical parent assumes his or her child will drink during high school. Studies show that's a fair assumption: 80 percent will at least have tried alcohol by the time they graduate. Studies also show, however, that 53 percent of parents think there's nothing they can do about it. Wallace calls this the "myth of inevitability" and he says it's just plain wrong.

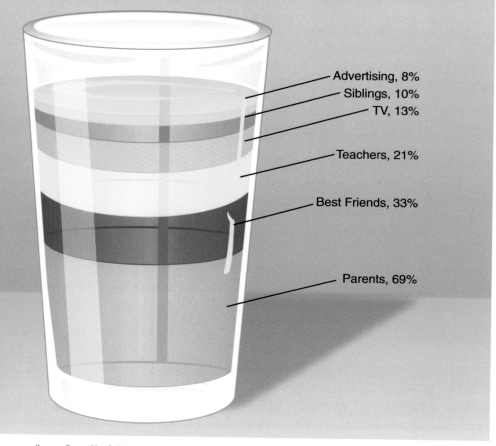

Influences on Teen Drinking, as Viewed by Youths Age 13–17

Advertising, 8%
Siblings, 10%
TV, 13%
Teachers, 21%
Best Friends, 33%
Parents, 69%

Source: Roper Youth Report, a nationwide cross-section syndicated survey of 544 8- to 17-year-olds. Based on responses of 13- to 17-year-olds. Note: Numbers do not add up to 100 percent because more than one response was accepted.

"Our research shows parents can have extraordinary influence," he says.

Even though teens may say they don't want to hear what parents have to say, they don't mean it, says Wallace. "When you back off," he says, "kids conclude, 'My parents don't really care if I drink, so I will.'" Teenagers whose parents talk to them frequently about alcohol report that when they are faced with a decision to drink or not, or to take the second or third drink, they often hear a parent's voice in their head. In other words, says Wallace, conversations can be deterrents.

Start having those talks when your children are in elementary school, says Kulig. (He fears the newest figures from the Monitoring the Future study will show drinking is beginning even earlier than eighth grade.) "It's much better when communication is part of normal interactions than if you wait until something bad happens," he says. Besides, the younger children are when you start the conversations, the more likely they are to absorb your values.

Points to Convey

There are three important points to convey:

Alcohol is an adult beverage unlike any other because it can make you act differently than you normally do, including stupidly.

Adults can drink a little and be OK, but you have to be an adult to be able to make that judgment.

If you drink, talk about why you do and how you keep it under control. If you have a problem, or someone in your family does, be honest. Studies show children of alcoholics are not only genetically predisposed but also at risk because of their socialization to it.

With teenagers, Kulig says, "It's a terrible idea when parents think, 'They'll drink anyway, let them do it here and be safe.' All that does is condone inappropriate behavior. Remember the 17-year-old girl who died in 1998?" She drank 15 beers at a friend's North Andover [Massachusetts] home and then fell down the basement stairs and cracked her skull. The friend's father had supplied the alcohol.

It helps to give teenagers reasons why they shouldn't drink, not just orders not to: "I love you and I care about you and I don't want you to drink because it could impair your judgment, or damage brain cells, or affect your memory forever." Believe it or not, says Wallace, teenagers like it when parents rehearse refusal skills with them. ("I have a blood disorder, I can't drink") and rescue plans (a teenager who calls home and asks, "Did grandpa have to go to the hospital?" is code for, "Come get me, no questions asked.")

Be Awake and Set Limits

Perhaps the single most important tip for parents is to be awake to greet your teenager when she comes home at night, what Wallace calls "the tough duty." It's not so much that a teen will debrief with you, although some will; more importantly, it's a deterrent to know she has to face you. It's also a way to pick up clues: Does she smell from alcohol? Is her speech slurred? If she does come home intoxicated (or even just smelling of beer), give her whatever help she needs and save a conversation for the next day. Otherwise, you're likely to impose consequences you can't or won't enforce ("You're grounded for the rest of the year"), which tells her it isn't really a big deal.

As with any misbehaviors, the best limits are ones that are clearly defined before the fact; with teenagers, they also are negotiated, not imposed. Wallace thinks one reason parents aren't clear enough about alcohol and drug behavior is that we feel compromised by our own teenage indiscretions. "What you did is irrelevant," he tells parents. "Your job now is to help your child make safe decisions."

The responsibility for keeping teenagers safe does not rest solely with parents. Ralph Hingson, associate dean for research at the School of Public Health at Boston University and lead author of a major college drinking study released two weeks ago [in April 2002], urges parents to connect with other parents, and to work in the community to push for stronger seat-belt law enforcement and increased community education and enforcement.

Spring is a time of year, for instance, when teenage drinking increases. Are you talking to parents of friends about their policy on alcohol? About party supervision? Do you have an agreement to call a parent if a child is intoxicated? Many parents and communities are extra vigilant on prom or graduation night. What about tonight?

EVALUATING THE AUTHORS' ARGUMENTS:

The viewpoint you just read is written by a journalist who uses quotes by medical experts to support her conclusion that parents can influence their teenage children's decisions abut drinking. In the next viewpoint, a parent describes his own inability to prevent his teenage son from drinking in order to make the point that parental influence is limited. Which approach do you find more persuasive, and why?

Parents Have Limited Influence over Teens' Drinking Behavior

Dympna Ugwu-Oju

"Good parenting can only go so far in shaping our children's decisions."

Dympna Ugwu-Oju is an instructor at the Madera Center of the State Center Community College District in Madera, California. In the following viewpoint he describes his dismay at discovering that his teenage son has experimented with alcohol. Ugwu-Oju insists that he has been an attentive and involved parent who has endeavored to teach his son the harms of alcohol and steer him away from making the wrong decisions about drinking. Moreover, he contends that his son is a responsible teenager who gets good grades and respects adults. Despite all his efforts, Ugwu-Oju maintains, he was unable to prevent his son from succumbing to peer pressure. Based on his experience, the author concludes that the impact parents have on their children's decision to drink is limited.

AS YOU READ, CONSIDER THE FOLLOWING QUESTIONS:
1. Why was Ugwu-Oju confident that his son would not drink?
2. How much money does underage drinking cost society each year, according to the statistic cited by the author?

M y best friend and I just learned that our teen-age sons have been experimenting with alcohol. We are still in shock. We never thought that our children would succumb under pressure from their peers or the lure of popular culture.

My friend and I had believed that a child's behavior reflects his parents, and that a child strays because his parents failed him somehow. It seemed that simple: Good parents raise responsible children. Now I know better, and, as much as I detest admitting it, I understand how good parenting can only go so far in shaping our children's decisions.

Until I learned of my son's involvement, I had believed that my children were immune to the epidemic of rebelliousness that plagues American teen-agers and that they had immense respect for us, themselves and authority to keep them safe. I had no reason to think otherwise. They are brilliant students, articulate, involved in school and community activities, and very respectful of their parents, teachers, other adults and especially themselves.

FAST FACT

A survey conducted by Peter D. Hart Research Associates found that 31 percent of parents believed their teens had consumed an alcoholic beverage. A survey of teens themselves found that a much larger number—60 percent— had actually consumed alcohol.

"All the Perks"

My friend and I share the same philosophy about raising children and, until the discovery, we had both accepted the general misconception of the types of children who would experiment with alcohol and drugs. Our children do not fit the stereotype. They enjoy all the perks of upper middle class America: professional parents with strong marriages; homes in safe and stable neighborhoods; schools that

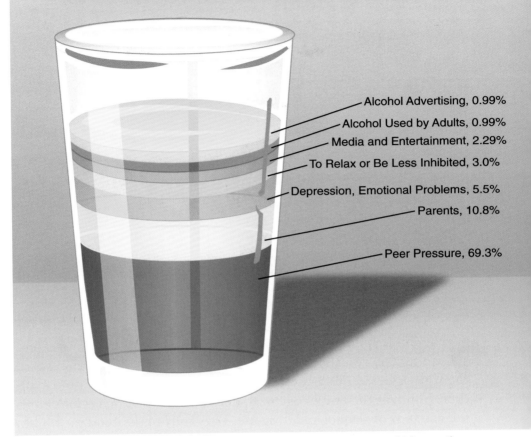

Causes of Underage Drinking as Viewed by Adults

Alcohol Advertising, 0.99%
Alcohol Used by Adults, 0.99%
Media and Entertainment, 2.29%
To Relax or Be Less Inhibited, 3.0%
Depression, Emotional Problems, 5.5%
Parents, 10.8%
Peer Pressure, 69.3%

Source: Taken from a survey of 900 adults conducted by the National Center on Addiction and Substance Abuse as reported in *Teen Tipplers: America's Underage Drinking Epidemic,* February 2002.

are carefully chosen to prepare them for successful careers; friends whose families share traditional values; and adult role models who are highly reputable. In addition, our children are growing up in material and spiritual abundance. They attend church, take religious classes every week and have a good grasp of the scriptures.

We were quite confident that our well-bred children would never participate in teen-age drinking, drug use or other aberrant teen-age behavior. They are after all, children of privilege—with enough self-confidence to withstand peer pressure, intelligent enough to know better, moral enough to always choose right over wrong and clever enough to not break the law deliberately.

Parents gather to demonstrate the dangers of drinking and driving. It is estimated that 80 percent of high school students will use alcohol by the time they graduate.

Our children know all the facts. We've both engaged them in extensive discussions on the evils of drinking or doing drugs and exposed them to assorted literature detailing these ills. Any one of our children could, at the tender age of 8, deliver a compelling argument on the demerits of alcohol and drug use. They fully understood the health, mental, social and legal implications.

My friend and I were firm but very hands-on in our parenting and stayed fully involved in all our children's activities. We kept television sets turned off, filled our homes with books and planned our days around the children's programs. Sadly, we operated under the misguided notion that our children's choices would be shaped more by the lessons we taught them than outside influences.

But we were wrong, completely wrong. The reality is that our children, like 80% of American high school students, will use alcohol by the time they graduate from high school, even though they know we do not approve or condone such behavior. According to one study, there may be more than 4 million American alcoholics under the age of 18, and as many as 79% of teen-agers say being drunk is appealing because "it feels good."

Part of the Crowd

My friend's son said he drank out of curiosity and because everyone was drinking and he didn't want to be the odd man out. But no matter what the reasons are, statistics prove that American teen-agers are drinking alcohol excessively, a behavior that is both dangerous and damaging to them. According to a 1999 study by the Centers for Disease Control, millions of children start drinking before they turn 13. Of those teen-agers who admitted using alcohol before their 13th birthday, 35.2% are African-American, 35.1% are Hispanic, and 29.9% are Caucasian. Underage drinking costs our society approximately $453 billion annually.

Parents should know that whether we admit to it or not, alcohol use is the No. 1 drug problem among young people. In 2000, California recorded 498 alcohol-related vehicle deaths for 15- to 20-year-olds. Nationwide, 6,390 young men and women died in car crashes caused by their own drinking or the drinking of someone else. Sixty-three percent

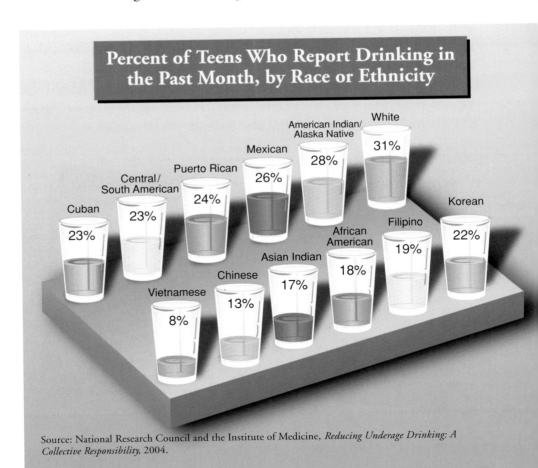

Percent of Teens Who Report Drinking in the Past Month, by Race or Ethnicity

White 31%

American Indian/ Alaska Native 28%

Mexican 26%

Puerto Rican 24%

Central/ South American 23%

Cuban 23%

Korean 22%

Filipino 19%

African American 18%

Asian Indian 17%

Chinese 13%

Vietnamese 8%

Source: National Research Council and the Institute of Medicine, *Reducing Underage Drinking: A Collective Responsibility,* 2004.

of youth who died in passenger vehicle crashes were not wearing seat belts, and fatally injured drivers who have been drinking are least likely to have been wearing safety belts. An average of one teen-ager dies each hour in a car crash during a typical weekend. More than 45% of crashes of cars driven by teen-agers involved alcohol.

Numerous Pitfalls

Sixty-six percent of boys and 64% of girls engage in at least one high-risk drinking activity over the course of a year. Alcohol use is also associated with early sexual activity as well as unprotected sex. Teen-age drinkers are more likely to progress to drug use, to show decline in academic performance and to drop out of school.

Our intellectual sons knew all that, but that knowledge and desire to please their parents were not enough deterrents. I wonder about other parents like us who did all the right things only to have their voices drowned by other more appealing and immediately gratifying influences.

Our sons assure us they would avoid all destructive behavior from now on. I have no reason not to believe them, but I am more aware of how feeble our voices must sound next to the other powers that hold their interest.

Meanwhile, I hope that other parents won't judge us as harshly as we did the parents of children who marched to the beats of a different drum. Now I know. It's not the parents; it's the children.

EVALUATING THE AUTHORS' ARGUMENTS:

The previous two authors, Barbara F. Meltz and Dympna Ugwu-Oju, both cite the statistic that 80 percent of high school students will try alcohol by the time they graduate. Based on this fact, do you think drinking is inevitable for most high school students? Do you think parents can have much of an influence over teens' decision to drink? Explain your answers.

Youths' Exposure to Alcohol Ads Should Be Limited

James A. O'Hara III

"We have found widespread . . . overexposure of underage youth to alcohol advertising."

James A. O'Hara III is the executive director of the Center on Alcohol Marketing and Youth, an organization that monitors the alcohol industry's advertising and marketing practices and their impact on young people. The following viewpoint was excerpted from O'Hara's testimony at a September 2003 Senate hearing on underage drinking. O'Hara argues that children and teenagers are exposed to too many alcohol advertisements. He contends that the industry places ads in magazines, during television shows, and on radio stations that have a high proportion of underage audiences. In response, O'Hara calls on the alcohol industry to place ads where the underage audience is 15 percent or less.

James A. O'Hara III, statement before the U.S. Senate Subcommittee on Substance Abuse and Mental Health Services, Committee on Health, Education, Labor, and Pensions, Washington, DC, September 30, 2003.

Responsibility for alcohol advertising rests with the [alcohol] industry. The industry regulates itself through the codes of the trade associations and of individual companies. In general, these codes address two main topics: content and placement. Over the years, the content of alcohol advertising has generated some of the sharpest controversy in terms of questions of its appeal to underage youth. The Budweiser frogs and Spuds McKenzie may be two of the most well-known and controversial. A 1996 study of children ages nine to 11 found that children were more familiar with Budweiser's television frogs than Kellogg's Tony the Tiger, the Mighty Morphin Power Rangers, or Smokey the Bear. Even the most recent FTC [Federal Trade Commission] report that commended the industry for "added . . . attention to the issue of ad content" also remarked, "Still, a visible minority of beer ads feature concepts that risk appealing to those under 21." . . .

The Center's [the Center on Alcohol Marketing and Youth (CAMY)] primary focus, however, has been on the placement of alcohol advertising—where the industry chooses to place its ads, and who is exposed to the advertising and how frequently. . . . Since September 2002 we have released a series of reports on the exposure of underage youth—ages 12 to 20—to alcohol advertising in the measured media of magazines, television and radio. Our research has, in effect, been an attempt to conduct public health surveillance of alcohol advertising, using the databases routinely used by advertising agencies and consumer product companies in the planning of advertising campaigns. To assist us in this effort, we have employed the services of Virtual Media Resources, a media research and planning firm based in Natick, Massachusetts.

Youth Are Overexposed

We have found widespread and pervasive overexposure of underage youth to alcohol advertising in all three media.

For magazines: Youth saw more beer and distilled spirits advertising than adults in magazines in 2001—45 percent more for beer brands and 27 percent more for distilled spirits brands.

Marketers of low-alcohol refreshers, the so-called "malternatives" such as Smirnoff Ice, delivered 60 percent more magazine advertising to youth than adults in 2001.

These ads have been placed in magazines like *Vibe* and *Spin* that, respectively, had underage audiences of 41 percent and 39 percent in 2001, as well as in magazines like *Allure* with a 34 percent underage audience and *In Style* with 2.5 percent underage readership.

Television and Radio

For television: Almost a quarter of the television alcohol advertising in 2001—51,084 ads—was more likely to be seen by youth than by adults.

Dean Smith, the former head basketball coach of the University of North Carolina, speaks at a 2003 press conference about a campaign to restrict alcohol advertising at college sporting events.

In 2001, alcohol advertising on television reached 89 percent of young people 12–20, who saw an average of 246 alcohol ads each. The 30 percent of young people ages 12–20 who were most likely to see alcohol advertising on television saw at least 780 alcohol TV ads in 2001.

The alcohol industry's television advertising has been placed on shows like *That '70s Show, The Parkers,* and *MADtv.*

For radio: Youth heard more radio advertising for beer, "malternatives" and distilled spirits in 2001 and 2002 than adults 21 and over. Underage youth, ages 12–20, heard 8 percent more beer and ale advertising and 12 percent more malternative advertising. The exposure was even greater for the distilled spirits category, where youth heard 14 percent more advertising.

The vast majority of radio advertising reaching underage youth was placed on radio stations with four formats: Rhythmic Contemporary Hit, Pop Contemporary Hit, Urban Contemporary and Alternative. The artists featured on these formats are, for example, 50 Cent, Jennifer Lopez, LL Cool J, Nelly, Justin Timberlake, Eminem, Ja Rule, Dru Hill, Snoop Dogg, Red Hot Chili Peppers, Audioslave and Foo Fighters. . . .

How to Protect Youth

Our research has utilized the most current data available to provide a reliable and verifiable analysis of underage youth exposure to alcohol advertising. The key public policy question going forward is how we

Source: Barnett. © by Jerry Barnett. Reproduced by permission.

protect underage youth from excessive exposure to alcohol advertising. It should be kept in mind that the alcohol industry has already agreed that there should be some limits to their advertising by the very fact that for years they have had voluntary codes restricting the placement of their own advertising.

The IOM [Institute of Medicine] report [*Reducing Underage Drinking: A Collective Responsibility*] also lays out what we believe is a convincing public policy rationale for limits on the alcohol advertising that reaches underage youth:

It is sometimes assumed that, in the absence of compelling evidence of causation, there is no legitimate basis for limiting the exposure of young people to alcohol advertising. This assumption is wrong for three reasons. First, the absence of definitive proof may be caused by the methodological complexity of the inquiry rather than the absence of a contributing effect. . . . Second, there is a sound common sense basis for believing, even in the absence of definitive proof, that making alcohol use attractive to young people increases the likelihood that they will become alcohol consumers as young people rather than waiting until they are adults. . . . Third, persistent exposure of young people to messages *encouraging* drinking by young people (even if they appear to be 21) contradicts and interferes with the implementation of the nation's goal of *discouraging* underage drinking.

The last point made by IOM deserves underlining: the alcohol industry's advertising of the good times to be had by the consumption of alcohol undercuts and drowns out the messages of responsibility and caution given by parents and other adults. And parents know this and want something done. We commissioned public opinion research by Peter D. Hart Associates and American Viewpoint

Some advocates argue that the alcohol industry should limit the number of alcohol advertisements young people are exposed to.

and found that parents overwhelmingly (81 percent) believe that, due to the potentially harmful effects of its products, the alcohol industry has a special responsibility to avoid exposing young people to messages encouraging alcohol consumption.

A 15 Percent Threshold Is Needed

The beer and distilled spirits industries, as of this month [September 2003] according to the recent [2003] FTC report and their own trade associations, have now committed not to place alcohol advertising where the underage audience is 30 percent or more. This is a significant reduction from the previous industry threshold of 50 percent and is to be welcomed. Whether it is sufficiently protective of our children remains the question, however.

The IOM has recommended that industry move toward a 15 percent threshold, and CAMY's own research suggests a 15 percent threshold is the most protective and likely to prevent routine overexposure of underage youth, ages 12 to 20. The reasoning is straightforward. Underage youth represent 15.8 percent of the U.S. population, age 12 and over. Advertising placed in venues where the audience composition is 15 percent or less simply follows the distribution of the population. As I said, the IOM has called for the industry to move toward this threshold. In addition, when a distilled spirits company sought to break the decades-old voluntary ban on distilled spirits advertising on broadcast television, it proposed to limit its advertising to late-night television, and in other dayparts to limit its advertising to programs where the underage audience was 15 percent or less. Also, the company promised to air one of its responsibility ads for every four product ads. Finally, a representative for the leading beer company in the United States—Anheuser Busch—was recently quoted as saying the "vast majority" of their advertising in the last 10 years has been placed on programs "which traditionally attract audiences that are approximately 80 percent adult." Clearly, what needs to happen is a balancing of the public health goal of limiting underage youth exposure to alcohol advertising and of the rightful economic self-interest of alcohol companies to advertise to their legal audience. With a distilled spirits company indicating that a 15 percent threshold is economically viable and with the country's largest beer company saying that a "vast majority" of its advertising has met a 20 percent threshold for the last 10 years, it would appear that some reduction from the newly announced 30 percent threshold, which allows for placement of alcohol ads where underage youth are twice their number in the general population, is still achievable and would further the public health goal.

EVALUATING THE AUTHOR'S ARGUMENTS:

In the viewpoint you just read, the author cites various magazines and television shows that he says contain numerous ads for alcoholic products. Do you read these magazines and watch these shows? Do you believe you are overexposed to alcohol advertisements? If so, do you believe they have an adverse effect on you? Why or why not?

Youths' Exposure to Alcohol Ads Is Adequately Limited

Jeff Becker

"[Beer companies] voluntarily . . . avoid advertising and marketing that could be perceived as directed at youth."

Jeff Becker is the president of the Beer Institute, an organization that promotes the interests of the beer industry. The following viewpoint is excerpted from testimony he delivered to a Senate hearing investigating the issue of underage drinking in the United States. Becker rejects the charge that alcohol advertising and marketing targets children and teens. Rather, he insists that the industry regulates itself in a responsible manner in order to promote its products to adult consumers. As evidence of the industry's commitment to shield young people from inappropriate messages, he cites the industry's decision to advertise its products only to audiences that are at least 70 percent adult.

AS YOU READ, CONSIDER THE FOLLOWING QUESTIONS:

1. What is the most important influence in preventing underage drinking, according to Becker?

Jeff Becker, statement before the U.S. Senate Subcommittee on Substance Abuse and Mental Health Services, Committee on Health, Education, Labor, and Pensions, Washington, DC, September 30, 2003.

2. What were the results of the 2003 Federal Trade Commission report, as cited by the author?
3. What was the conclusion of the National Academies of Science report cited by Becker?

I am pleased to represent almost 900,000 men and women employed by our [beer] industry. . . . Our industry has a long and proud tradition of giving back to the communities where we live and do business, and we share the commitment of the members of this Subcommittee [Senate Subcommittee on Substance Abuse and Mental Health Services] to combat illegal underage drinking.

Our commitment stems from two areas. First, it is no surprise to learn that many in our ranks are parents themselves—they share the concerns of all parents in this regard. But equally important, we do not like to see illegal underage consumption of the products that our members take such great care to make for adults of legal purchase age. We are joined in our commitment to be part of the solution to

These beer cans feature the Super Bowl XXXIX logo. Some alcohol manufacturers have come under fire for such marketing, which critics say appeals to young people.

underage drinking by a large percentage of small and large business-es in the United States that would not be successful without a license to sell alcohol beverages. I can assure you that we have enlisted the commitment and the talents of personnel from our member compa-nies, beer wholesalers, and retailers across the nation in the ongoing challenges posed by illegal underage drinking. We do not want the business of young people below the legal purchase age. . . .

Parents Are the Key Influence

A critical area in which I believe we have broad societal agreement is the importance of active parental involvement to prevent underage drink-ing. Brewers have long advocated and sponsored programs to facilitate parental discussions about drinking with their young children as well as their college-bound teens. By acknowledging the temptation associated with underage drinking and encouraging their children to respect them-selves and the law, parents can make an enormous difference. Brewer materials for parents are available in five languages with useful infor-mation to explain why drinking is inappropriate for youth. These efforts are effective because they draw on the strong influence par-ents have over their children's deci-sions about drinking.

> ## FAST FACT
>
> In a survey conducted by the University of Minnesota, 67.2 percent of respondents favored banning hard liquor ads from television. More than 58 percent favored banning beer and wine ads.

For over a decade, according to a national poll conducted by the Roper Research organization, youth have identified their parents as the most powerful influence in their decision to drink or to refrain from drinking. I should point out that advertising has always been one of the choices offered in the survey. Every year, it has ranked dead last as an influential factor by the most important group in this discus-sion: youths themselves.

Because young people have so plainly told us that parents are the most effective way to reach them on the issue of underage drinking, we strong-ly believe in providing information and encouragement to help parents exercise this influence. And we do. Over the last several years, our mem-

Many people argue that strong parental involvement is key to controlling underage drinking.

bers have distributed over 5 million pieces of material—guidebooks, videos, and others—to parents across the U.S. Brewers have also maintained on-going national advertising campaigns and comprehensive websites dedicated to this issue. . . .

Advertising Responsibly

Since our industry's advertising activities have recently been the subject of Congressional interest, I would like to briefly touch on some other developments that underscore our commitment to market and sell our products to adults of legal purchase age. The FTC's [Federal

Trade Commission] 2003 Report unequivocally stated that beer industry members do not target underage consumers. Critics seek to use advertising as a lightning rod to divert attention from the real issues. Perhaps it is because they question the larger issue of beer's respected place in American society. But let's face it: drinking beer is not the only adult activity that youth should not engage in. In fact, this is just one of the many rules that society imposes on young people as they pass through maturity on their way to adulthood. And the most effective way to keep youth from engaging in adult behavior is not to pretend that adult products don't exist or that advertising causes people under 21 to drink. The way to address this issue is to help youth navigate through an adult world where there are many things—driving a car, voting in an election—not just drinking, that are not appropriate for them until they reach an age of maturity.

FAST FACT

The Beer Institute's voluntary advertising marketing code states that beer ads should not contain imagery that appeals mainly to people under twenty-one, including depictions of Santa Claus. It also states that actors and models used in beer advertising should be at least twenty-five years old and that beer should not be advertised at events where most attendees are under twenty-one.

At the same time, our advertising is intended for adults, and our members voluntarily undertake extensive steps to avoid advertising and marketing that could be perceived as directed at youth. Self-regulation in this area is very important from a public policy perspective.

The 2003 FTC report further reinforces a statement from a 1999 agency report on alcohol beverage advertising: "Self-regulation is a realistic, responsive and responsible approach to many of the issues raised by underage drinking. It can deal quickly and flexibly with a wide range of advertising issues and brings the accumulated experience and judgment of an industry to bear without the rigidity of government regulations." The FTC has conducted four comprehensive reviews of industry advertising practices over the last five years. The FTC recently indicated that, "Self-regulation practices in the alcohol industry have shown improvement since issuance of the 1999 Report. . . ." Its September 2003 report cited improvements in the area of ad placement, noting that industry members had shown 99% compliance with industry standards governing placement of broadcast advertising. The FTC report discusses a number of important changes in our industry advertising code, which I will touch on in a moment. In the interest of full disclosure, the FTC also included some cautionary comments about advertising content and other issues, and we take the Commission's advice seriously.

In addition to the latest FTC report, the National Academies [of Science] report to Congress [*Reducing Underage Drinking: A Collective Responsibility*] recognized the importance of self-regulation. The report does highlight the age-old scholarly debate over advertising and underage drinking, which clearly indicates that advertising is not a significant factor in underage drinking or the decision to drink at any age. Beyond that discussion, however, the National Academies panel states, "The industry has the prerogative—indeed, the social obligation—to regulate its own practices in promotional activities that have a particular appeal to youngsters, irrespective of whether such practices can be *proven* to 'cause' underage drinking." [emphasis in original] . . .

For over 50 years, Beer Institute's members have maintained socially responsible business practices including a policy of vigorous self-regulation of advertising and marketing. First adopted in 1943, the

Many people argue that the alcohol industry cannot be held accountable for such serious societal problems as underage drinking and driving.

beer industry's advertising code has evolved over time to respond to societal and technological developments. We want our intentions to be clear to our consumers as well as to those who do not drink. Our primary goal as an industry is to reach out to those who can legally purchase our products with tasteful, contemporary advertising that increases awareness of our members' brands. Our ads are enjoyed by millions of Americans and rated highly in numerous surveys of adult consumers. Consistent with our long-standing policies, the Beer Institute Code was recently revised to incorporate some of the best practices of our member companies and to address several FTC recommendations.

I am pleased to inform you that our members have revised the standard for advertising placements in television, radio, and magazines to require placements only where the proportion of the audience above age 21 is reasonably expected to be 70% or higher. This standard reflects the demographics of the U.S. population, in which approximately 70% of the public is age 21 or older. We have also expanded our code provisions covering marketing at or near college campuses and product placement in television programs and movies. . . .

In closing, I'd like to leave you with this last fact. Brewers fully recognize that underage drinking is a problem that our society must embrace and tackle. We hope that we will be given the consideration to be a meaningful part of that fight, through our demonstrated commitment to this issue. As the father of two children, I share this committee's concern—just like every other parent out there.

EVALUATING THE AUTHORS' ARGUMENTS:

This chapter contains several proposed methods of preventing underage drinking. Rank these methods in order of most effective to least effective and explain your rationale for your choices.

CHAPTER 3

How Can Drunk Driving Be Reduced?

A police officer gives a sobriety test to a suspected drunk driver.

VIEWPOINT 1

Minimum Drinking-Age Laws Reduce Drunk Driving

Steven Chapman

"The higher drinking age saves about 1,000 lives a year."

Prior to 1988, states were free to determine their own legal drinking age. In 1988, Congress passed a law requiring states to set their minimum legal drinking age at twenty-one in order to receive federal highway funds. In the following viewpoint Steven Chapman argues that this law has led to a reduction in drunk driving by young motorists. The minimum drinking age cannot entirely prevent drunk driving, he acknowledges, but it can deter a significant number of young people from obtaining alcohol and getting behind the wheel. Steven Chapman is a member of the editorial board of the *Chicago Tribune* newspaper.

AS YOU READ, CONSIDER THE FOLLOWING QUESTIONS:
1. How much did drunk driving among young people decrease during the time period studied by the Centers for Disease Control and Prevention, according to the author?
2. What special penalties have many states instituted to reduce drunk driving among youths, as reported by Chapman?
3. Why is twenty-one a better legal drinking age than eighteen, in the author's opinion?

Steven Chapman, "There's Some Safety in the Number 21," *Chicago Tribune,* December 8, 2002, p. 11.

Jenna and Barbara Bush [the daughters of President George W. Bush] recently turned 21, which means two things: They can drink legally wherever liquor is served, and the Secret Service can breathe a sigh of relief.

Probably the only presidential daughters to be sentenced to community service for underage drinking violations, the Bush twins will no longer have to figure out ways to circumvent the drinking age. But they should be grateful for the law that caused them so much trouble—because without it, they might not be around for this passage to adulthood.

In 2001 Jenna (left) and Barbara Bush were arrested and sentenced to community service for underage drinking.

The Bush daughters were cited by Austin [Texas] police last year [2001] for doing what a lot of teenagers do—Barbara for being a minor in possession of alcohol and Jenna for using a fake ID to buy a drink. The incident provoked a lot of complaints about the injustice of 19-year-olds being granted virtually every right enjoyed by adults except free access to booze. The British magazine *The Economist* for example, ridiculed our drinking age as a product of "petty Puritanism and a pathological obsession with safety."

This squares with the obvious interests of the brewing industry. A couple of years ago, August Busch III, chairman of Anheuser-Busch, said, "We need to listen to those who say that a law that makes it illegal for college students to drink a beer is wrong and that it results in the very behavior we are trying to fight." Peter Coors, who heads a brewery of the same name, once voiced similar sentiments.

FAST FACT

According to the National Center on Addiction and Substance Abuse at Columbia University, 84 percent of teens and 83 percent of adults favor a minimum drinking age of twenty-one.

An Effective Law

But what's good for Anheuser-Busch isn't necessarily what's good for young people. The evidence about what happened when states raised the drinking age from 18 to 21 is as clear as those Rocky Mountain streams you see in the Coors ads: The carnage on the highways greatly subsided.

A new report from the federal Centers for Disease Control and Prevention [CDC] dramatizes the results of setting the drinking age at 21. Alcohol-related traffic deaths among all groups have fallen substantially over the last two decades—thanks largely to tougher law enforcement and changing social attitudes. But the biggest decline has come among the youngest motorists.

Among drivers age 16–17, says the CDC, the rate of crashes involving a driver who has been drinking plunged by 60 percent. For 18-to-20-year-olds, they dropped by 55 percent. Among those above age 25, by contrast, the decline was just 39 percent. Since 1999, fatality rates have risen a bit for every age group—except 16- and 17-year-olds.

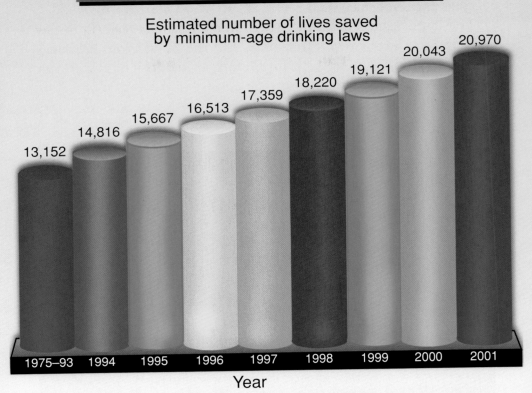

Minimum-Age Drinking Laws Save Lives

Estimated number of lives saved
by minimum-age drinking laws

1975–93	1994	1995	1996	1997	1998	1999	2000	2001
13,152	14,816	15,667	16,513	17,359	18,220	19,121	20,043	20,970

Year

Source: *Traffic Safety Facts 2001: Alcohol,* National Highway Traffic Safety Administration, National Center for Statistics and Analysis, Washington, DC, 2001.

Our "pathological obsession with safety" has done much to extend the life expectancy of teenagers. Chuck Hurley, vice president of the National Safety Council, says the data indicate that the higher drinking age saves about 1,000 lives a year. Drinking and driving used to be the leading cause of death among teenagers. Not anymore.

Reasons for Progress

What accounts for the progress? There's an obvious explanation: Those under 21 can no longer buy liquor legally. All states were required to raise their drinking age by 1988 as a condition of getting federal highway funds.

Another reason is that most states now mandate special penalties for kids caught drinking and driving—even if they're not drunk. A minor caught with even low levels of alcohol in his blood may suffer an automatic license suspension, which serves as a powerful deterrent against reckless behavior.

Let's not overstate the impact of the higher drinking age. Alas, not all teenagers have sworn off alcohol. But the 21-year-old rule does pose something of an obstacle for minors, as the Bush daughters can attest.

As part of an effort to curb drunk driving, state legislatures throughout the United States have made it unlawful to drive with open containers of alcohol in the vehicle.

It has certainly been one factor in the steady decline in alcohol consumption among teens. In 1979, the federal government reports, half of all kids from age 12 to 17 drank regularly. Today the figure is 18.6 percent. Consumption has also declined among those age 18 to 20.

Now, kids of 16 or 17 weren't allowed to purchase alcohol even before the drinking age was raised.

But setting the floor at 21 instead of 18 creates a bigger hurdle for high school kids, because they're less likely to have friends old enough to buy for them. Most adolescents say it's harder to buy beer than it is to get marijuana.

The zero-tolerance laws assure that even kids who do drink will think twice, or three times, before getting behind the wheel. For a 16-year-old, the prospect of losing her license for six months sounds like a life sentence at hard labor in Alcatraz. Most teenagers prize their driving privileges even more than they like drinking, so they generally take care not to mix the two.

As a result, a lot more of them are living to see their 21st birthday. For Jenna and Barbara, the 21-year-old drinking age may be a blessing very well disguised. But a blessing it is.

EVALUATING THE AUTHOR'S ARGUMENTS:

In the viewpoint you just read, the author quotes a British magazine, the *Economist*, which said that the U.S. minimum drinking age is the result of America's "petty Puritanism and a pathological obsession with safety." Do you think the *Economist* has a point? Why or why not?

VIEWPOINT 2

Minimum Drinking-Age Laws Do Not Reduce Drunk Driving

Ed Quillen

"A lower drinking age doesn't mean more highway deaths."

In the following viewpoint, Ed Quillen rejects the argument that raising the drinking age to twenty-one has reduced drunk driving. As evidence, he compares statistics on driving fatalities in Colorado, where the drinking age is twenty-one, and Puerto Rico, which has a lower minimum drinking age. Based on this evidence, Quillen concludes that the minimum drinking-age law should be eliminated entirely. That way, he claims, children could learn about alcohol at an early age, and the glamour of drinking would be minimized. Ed Quillen is a former newspaper editor and a columnist for the *Denver Post* newspaper.

AS YOU READ, CONSIDER THE FOLLOWING QUESTIONS:

1. On what grounds is Jodie Pisco suing Coors Brewing Company, according to the author?

One place where America must lead the world is in bizarre litigation. A case in point was filed recently in Reno, Nev., where about two years ago [2002], Ryan Pisco died after drinking a lot of beer and driving his girlfriend's car into a lamppost at 90 mph. He was only 19, and the legal drinking age in Nevada, as in the rest of the United States, is 21.

Naturally, this death had to be the fault of someone other than Ryan; 19-year-olds may know enough to vote or deploy lethal weapons in Iraq, but apparently they can be controlled by pictures on television or in magazines.

An Unsupportable Case

That's the argument being advanced by Jodie Pisco, Ryan's mother. She is suing Coors Brewing Co. for the loss of her son, on the grounds that 'Coors sponsors and supports events that are attractive to minors

Alcohol manufacturers often sponsor sporting events such as this baseball game. Critics charge this type of advertising appeals to minors.

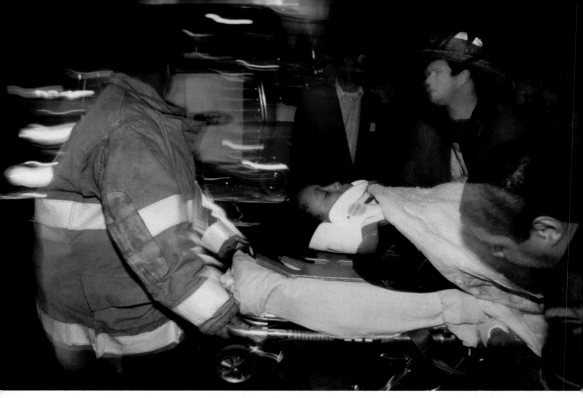

Paramedics tend to a person injured in a drunk-driving accident. Some argue that higher drinking ages do not result in fewer drunk-driving fatalities.

and youthful persons, glorifying a culture of youth, sex and glamor while hiding the dangers of alcohol abuse and addiction.'

Further, 'Coors targets the youth of America with false images of conquest, achievement and success that are reckless, willful and exhibit a deliberate disregard for the impact of illegal alcohol consumption by underage youths.'

Much of that is just legal boilerplate, and as for the rest, consider that most beer is consumed by young men in their 20s, and that breweries try to gain market share, rather than create new drinkers from teetotalers. If they are trying to increase consumption, they're doing a bad job of it: Annual per-capita beer consumption in this country declined from 24.3 gallons in 1980 to 21.7 gallons in 2000.

In case you're curious, per-capita consumption of wine and distilled spirits also fell in those two decades; Americans just don't drink as much as we used to.

And if they didn't market beer to 20-something guys, the ads would be even worse than they are now. How long would you watch a commercial that featured a bunch of half-bald gray-haired guys my age, all nursing beers while they grumbled about the Bush dynasty, the government in general, the war in Iraq, taxes, the economy and the like?

If we follow the logic of the Pisco argument, the brewery is somehow responsible for Ryan's death because it advertised to the people most likely to consume its product, and this made the product irresistible to people who weren't quite old enough to consume it legally.

That's a hard case to prove so I suspect this litigation will fail. But it probably won't be the last such effort.

Get Rid of the Minimum Drinking Age
Fortunately, the solution is simple: get rid of the minimum drinking age. Under the federal constitution, this is a state matter, as Congress has no authority. Congress got around this a few years ago by tying highway funds to drinking age—unless a state raised it to 21, then it would lose a percentage of the federal gasoline taxes its citizens had paid.

Colorado went along with it; before that, 18-year-olds could drink 3.2 beer. Puerto Rico didn't; to replace the lost tax revenue, the commonwealth installed toll booths along its major highways.

Source: Sharpnack. © 2003 by Joe Sharpnack. Reproduced by permission.

Yet the death rate from accidents in Puerto Rico in 1999 (the last year for which statistics are at hand) was 33.7 per 100,000 residents. That's lower than the U.S. average of 35.9 and the Colorado rate of 37.4.

So a lower drinking age doesn't mean more highway deaths. Many productive, civilized countries manage with a lower drinking age: no minimum in China or Portugal, 14 in Switzerland, 16 in most of Europe.

The idea here is to reduce the number of teenagers who drink and drive. If the drinking age were lowered to 16 or 18, it wouldn't help. Many kids start drinking at 16 because that's when they get their driving licenses, and that's when they can escape parental supervision.

Eliminate the minimum drinking age, and kids could learn all about alcohol long before they turned 16 and got their driver's license. Booze wouldn't seem like some glamorous adult activity.

Colorado could take the lead here, and eliminate the minimum drinking age. Statistics show that our highways would be just as safe, if not safer. And it would eliminate the possibility of lawsuits like the Pisco case; no company could be accused of targeting underage customers if there was no such thing.

EVALUATING THE AUTHORS' ARGUMENTS:

Steven Chapman and Ed Quillen both cite statistics to support their arguments about minimum drinking-age laws. Which author's statistics are more convincing? Defend your answer with specific examples from the viewpoints. After reading both viewpoints, what is your position on the issue? Do you think there should be a minimum legal drinking age? If so, what should the age be?

VIEWPOINT

3

Low Blood Alcohol Content Laws Reduce Drunk Driving

National Highway Traffic Safety Administration

".08 [blood alcohol concentration] laws . . . are associated with reductions in alcohol-related fatal crashes and fatalities."

The National Highway Traffic Safety Administration (NHTSA), a division of the U.S. Department of Transportation, is responsible for reducing deaths, injuries, and economic losses resulting from motor vehicle crashes. The following viewpoint is excerpted from an NHTSA report on laws that limit the amount of alcohol that drivers can have in their blood, which is known as the blood alcohol concentration (BAC). Prior to 2000, most states had laws that required motorists to remain below a .10 BAC, which meant that alcohol made up less than one-tenth of 1 percent of the driver's blood. In 2000, the federal government passed a law requiring states to lower the limit to .08 BAC or lose federal highway construction funds. Since then all fifty states have passed .08 BAC laws. The NHTSA applauds this change as a means of reducing the numbers of people killed in drunk-driving accidents.

National Highway Traffic Safety Administration, *Setting Limits, Saving Lives: The Case for .08 BAC Laws.* Washington, DC: U.S. Government Printing Office, April 2001.

AS YOU READ, CONSIDER THE FOLLOWING QUESTIONS:

1. What driving tasks are affected in a driver with a .08 BAC, according to the NHTSA?
2. What is the risk that an adult male between the ages of sixteen and twenty will crash if his BAC is between .08 and .10, as reported by the NHTSA?
3. What proportion of Americans will be involved in an alcohol-related crash at some time in their lives, according to the authors?

The amount of alcohol in a person's body is measured by the weight of the alcohol in a certain volume of blood. This is called the blood alcohol concentration, or "BAC." Because the volume of blood varies with the size of a person, BAC establishes an objective measure to determine levels of impairment.

The measurement is based on grams per deciliter (g/dl), and in most states a person is considered legally intoxicated if his or her BAC is .10 g/dl or greater; that is, alcohol makes up one-tenth of one percent of the person's blood.

A driver's BAC can be measured by testing the blood, breath, urine or saliva. Breath testing is the primary method used by law enforcement agencies. Preliminary breath testing can be performed easily during a roadside stop using a hand-held device carried by law enforcement officers. It is non-invasive and can even be performed while the person is still in his or her vehicle.

Evidentiary breath testing equipment is evaluated for precision and accuracy by NHTSA. Test instruments approved by NHTSA as conforming to specifications are accurate within plus or minus .005 of the true BAC value.

All states but one (Massachusetts) have established BAC *per se* levels. Twenty-four of those states plus the District of Columbia and Puerto Rico have set that level at .08. . . . [1]

Federal .08 BAC Law

In 1998, a plan was developed by NHTSA and its partners which encouraged states to promote and adopt a .08 BAC illegal *per se* limit,

---

1. A *per se* law makes it illegal in and of itself to drive with an alcohol concentration above the set limit. As of 2004, all fifty states had passed .08 BAC laws.

at or above which it is unlawful to drive a motor vehicle. The plan included: 1) setting a .08 BAC standard on federal property, including national parks and Department of Defense installations; 2) encouraging tribal governments to adopt, enforce, and publicize .08 BAC; and 3) developing an education campaign to help the public understand the risks associated with combining alcohol and driving. As a follow-up in November 1999, NHTSA published a status report of accomplishments to date on the .08 BAC national plan.

Legislation was first introduced in 1997 which would have required all states to enact and enforce .08 laws or face reductions in federal highway construction funds. In 1998 Congress passed the Transportation Equity Act for the 21st Century (TEA-21) authorizing highway, highway safety and other programs for the next six years. While TEA-21 did not establish .08 as the standard for impaired driving nationwide, it did provide $500 million of incentive grants over six years to states that have enacted and are enforcing a .08 *per se* law.

In October 2000, Congress passed .08 BAC as the national standard for impaired driving as part of the Transportation Appropriations Bill.

A San Francisco police officer gives a suspected drunk driver a Breathalyzer test in order to determine his blood alcohol content.

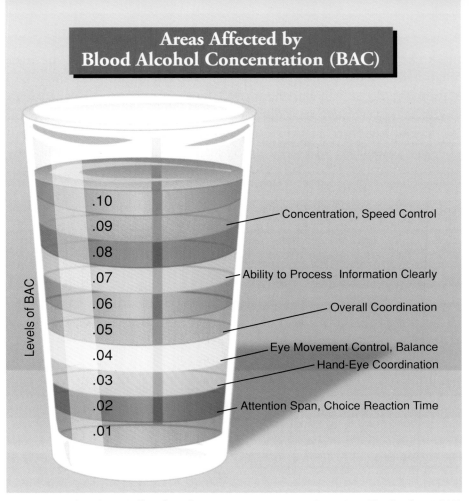

Areas Affected by Blood Alcohol Concentration (BAC)

Levels of BAC

.10
.09 — Concentration, Speed Control
.08
.07 — Ability to Process Information Clearly
.06 — Overall Coordination
.05
.04 — Eye Movement Control, Balance
— Hand-Eye Coordination
.03
.02 — Attention Span, Choice Reaction Time
.01

Source: National Highway Traffic Safety Administration, *Setting Limits, Saving Lives: The Case for .08 BAC Laws,* April 2001.

States that don't adopt .08 BAC laws by 2004 would have 2% of certain highway construction funds withheld, with the penalty increasing to 8% by 2007. States adopting the standard by 2007 would be reimbursed for any lost funds. This bill was signed on October 23, 2000. . . .

The Effect of Alcohol on Ability

With each drink consumed, a person's blood alcohol concentration increases. Although the outward appearances vary, virtually all drivers are substantially impaired at .08 BAC. Laboratory and on-road research shows that the vast majority of drivers, even experienced drinkers, are significantly impaired at .08 with regard to critical driving tasks such as braking, steering, lane changing, judgment and divided attention. In a recent study of 168 drivers, every one was significantly impaired with regard to at least one measure of driving performance at .08 BAC. The majority of drivers (60–94%) were impaired at .08 BAC in any one given measure. This is regardless of age, gender, or driving experience (see chart, "Areas Affected by Blood Alcohol Concentration (BAC)") . . . .

The risk of being in a motor vehicle crash also increases as the BAC level rises. The risk of being in a crash rises gradually with each BAC level, but then rises very rapidly after a driver reaches or exceeds .08 BAC compared to drivers with no alcohol in their system.

A recent NHTSA study indicates that between .08 and .10 BAC, the relative risk of a fatal single vehicle crash varied between 11% (drivers 35 and older) and 52% (male drivers age 16–20).

.08 Sets a Reasonable Limit

Setting the BAC limit at .08 is a reasonable response to the problem of impaired driving. At .08, virtually everyone is impaired to the point that driving skills are degraded. Research has provided clear and consistent evidence that .08 laws, particularly in combination with ALR [administrative license revocation] laws, are associated with reductions in alcohol-related fatal crashes and fatalities. Most states that have lowered their BAC to .08 have found a measurable drop in impaired driving fatalities, as have many industrialized countries that have adopted BAC limits of .08 and lower. .08 also impacts even heavy drinkers, who account for a high percentage of DWI [driving while intoxicated] arrests. At the same time, lowering the BAC limit to .08 makes it possible to convict seriously impaired drivers whose BAC levels would otherwise be considered marginal because they are at, or just over, .10.

> **FAST FACT**
>
> The National Highway Traffic Safety Administration estimates that implementing a .08 BAC law in Illinois caused a 13.7 percent decline in the number of fatal drunk-driving accidents.

The Case for .08 BAC Laws

The research is clear. Virtually all drivers are significantly impaired at .08 BAC. A 1988 NHTSA review of 177 studies documented this impairment. In 2000 NHTSA released a review of 112 more recent studies which provided additional evidence of impairment at .08 BAC. Thus nearly 300 studies have shown that, .08 BAC, virtually all drivers are impaired with regard to critical driving tasks such as divided attention, complex reaction time steering, lane changing and judgement.

A new comprehensive laboratory study provides what is perhaps the clearest laboratory evidence to date of the significant impairment that exists in all measures of performance by .08 BAC. In addition, this study finds that impairment exists in relatively equal levels among all age groups, sexes, and drinker types. This study, which employed a driving simulator and special divided attention test was conducted by the Southern California Research Institute, Human Factors North,

As blood alcohol content rises, the probability that a drunk driver will be involved in a crash increases dramatically.

and Westat Inc., all well-respected firms in the traffic safety research community.

Another reason for supporting .08 BAC laws is because they are effective in reducing alcohol-related fatal crashes. At least nine independent studies have now been conducted, covering nearly all of the states that have enacted .08 BAC laws. These studies have consistently shown that .08 BAC laws are associated with reductions in alcohol-related fatalities, particularly in conjunction with ALR laws. . . .

Impaired Driving Affects Us All

About two out of every five Americans will be involved in an alcohol-related crash at some time in their lives, and many of them will be innocent victims. There is no such thing as a drunk driving accident. Virtually all crashes involving alcohol could have been avoided if the impaired person were sober.

EVALUATING THE AUTHORS' ARGUMENTS:

The viewpoint you just read was produced by a department of the federal government that is charged with reducing motor vehicle crashes. The viewpoint that follows was written by the head of an organization that lobbies on behalf of the alcohol and restaurant industries. Does knowing this background affect your reading of the viewpoints? Why or why not? After reading both viewpoints, do you support lower BAC limits? Please defend your answer with references to the viewpoints.

Low Blood Alcohol Content Laws Do Not Reduce Drunk Driving

John Doyle

"Reducing the legal blood-alcohol concentration . . . won't lessen the drunk driving problem."

Blood alcohol concentration (BAC) laws forbid drivers from operating a vehicle when their blood contains more than a set legal limit of alcohol. As of 2004, all fifty states had BAC limits of .08 grams per deciliter. In the following viewpoint, John Doyle criticizes the efforts of advocacy groups—specifically Mothers Against Drunk Driving (MADD)—to lower the legal BAC level. According to Doyle, most drunk-driving accidents are caused by people with BAC levels well above the legal limit. Therefore, lowering the limit further will do nothing to solve the problem of drunk driving. Instead of lowering the BAC limits, Doyle concludes, anti–drunk driving advocates should focus their attention on preventing drunk-driving accidents by hard-core alcoholics. Doyle is the executive director of the

John Doyle, "MADD Is Reaching Too Far," *Cincinnati Post*, May 8, 2004, p. A14. Copyright © 2004 by *Cincinnati Post*. Reproduced by permission.

American Beverage Institute, a restaurant trade association that supports the responsible consumption of alcoholic beverages in the restaurant setting.

AS YOU READ, CONSIDER THE FOLLOWING QUESTIONS:
1. What has been the result of lowering the BAC limit from .10 to .08, according to the author?
2. What is the average BAC of drunken drivers involved in fatal accidents, as reported by Doyle?

I t started when you brought your kids to the restaurant. Anxiety began to set in when you ordered that single glass of wine. Driving home, you hit a police roadblock. And the courts took your kids away.

Sound like the trailer for a bad movie? It's actually a top priority for Mothers Against Drunk Driving. This previously admirable group has slipped into pure anti-alcohol zealotry with its "zero tolerance" campaign against drinking anything at all before driving. If you are a divorced parent who drives your kids safely home after having a single drink, MADD wants you to lose your parental rights. That's right, MADD wants this Prohibitionist requirement written into every separation agreement and divorce decree.

Ignoring the Real Problem

Reducing the legal blood-alcohol concentration, or BAC, arrest threshold to zero—whether for divorced parents or anyone else—may sound like a get-tough policy, but even MADD knows that won't lessen the drunk driving problem. During the last few years, nearly every state in the nation has reduced its BAC limit from .10 percent to .08 percent. The result? Drunk driving fatalities have actually increased.

The *Los Angeles Times* recently reported "some experts worry that new laws will actually reduce the attention placed on catching highly intoxicated drivers that cause the most deadly accidents." Indeed, the founder of MADD says "the movement I helped create has lost direction. (Lowering legal BAC limits) ignores the real core of the problem. . . . If we really want to save lives, let's go after the most dangerous drivers on the road."

Mothers Against Drunk Driving uses bumper stickers like these as one way to make the public aware of the importance of driving sober.

At their news conference announcing the zero tolerance policy for divorced parents, MADD highlighted two tragic cases where mothers killed or injured their children in alcohol-related accidents. Both women had a BAC approximately three times the legal limit. Clearly MADD's call for zero tolerance would have had no impact on these product abusers.

Drunken drivers involved in fatal accidents have an average BAC of .16 percent, which is already twice the legal limit in most states. To get that drunk, a 180 pound man would have to drink eight beers in one hour, or one drink every seven minutes. According to Herb Simpson, the winner of the National Commission Against Drunk Driving's 2003 "Humanitarian of the Year" Award, "These people don't have a glass of wine with dinner or a couple of beer(s). They're having 8, 10, 12, 14. . . ." Even MADD admits that the drunk driving problem has been reduced to a "hard core of alcoholics."

A Puritanical Effort

No one with an IQ above room temperature condones drunk driving, but it is absurd to equate alcohol abusers with the 25 million Americans who drink responsibly prior to driving. Scientific evidence proves that this legal behavior is far safer than driving while talking on a cell phone with a hands-free device. Studies from the University of Utah, the *New England Journal of Medicine* and elsewhere show that drivers using a hands-free cell phone are more "impaired" than drivers at .08 percent BAC.

Lowering BAC limits below the ubiquitous .08 percent will only fill our courtrooms with adults who, by current law and common sense, are driving responsibly.

So why would anyone want to focus law enforcement resources on a mom who had a glass of wine with dinner? Ideology. All too often, traffic safety policy has been hijacked by puritanical opponents of adult beverages. Utah recently passed a MADD-blessed law lowering BAC levels to .05 percent for repeat offenders with kids in the car. George Van Komen, who

> **FAST FACT**
>
> According to the National Highway Traffic Safety Administration, 65 percent of fatal drunk-driving deaths involve drivers whose BAC is .15 or higher.

co-wrote an original version of the law calling for .02 percent, opposes all alcohol consumption, period. He leads an organization formerly called the Anti-Saloon League and the National Temperance League.

Temperance is also on the tongue of MADD's highest officials. MADD President Wendy Hamilton recently wrote "the thought that

MADD president Wendy Hamilton speaks at a 2002 news conference. The group spends millions of dollars each year in its mission to put an end to drunk driving.

(driving) can be successfully combined with alcohol on the part of the driver or even the passengers defies any logic I can imagine." Even the passengers? Is MADD so anti-alcohol that they oppose designated drivers?

A lobbying behemoth, MADD has an annual budget of $46 million. It spends more than $12 million a year on salaries and benefits. Now that the drunk driving problem has been reduced to alcoholics who happily ignore their PR campaigns, MADD has become an institution in search of a mission. Its latest campaigns are demonstrative of its new cause: prohibition, drip by drip.

EVALUATING THE AUTHOR'S ARGUMENTS:

In the viewpoint you just read, John Doyle describes MADD as "a previously admirable group" that has "slipped into pure anti-alcohol zealotry." He also uses the words "puritanical," "temperance," and "prohibition" in reference to MADD. Does his use of these terms strengthen or weaken his arguments against MADD? Please explain.

FACTS ABOUT ALCOHOL

What Is Alcohol?

Alcohol is a drug that is categorized as a depressant. As such, it decreases the activity of the central nervous system and makes the user feel calm, entranced, and drowsy. In large doses it can cause drunkenness, a state of impaired physical and mental faculties.

Alcohol Abuse and Alcoholism

The National Institute on Alcohol Abuse and Alcoholism, an agency of the federal government, offers the following facts about alcohol abuse and alcoholism:

- Alcoholism is a disease with the following characteristics:
  - It is a chronic disease, meaning it lasts a person's lifetime.
  - It follows a predictable course.
  - It has the following four symptoms:
    1. Craving—A strong need, or urge, to drink
    2. Loss of control—Not being able to stop drinking once drinking has begun
    3. Physical dependence—Withdrawal symptoms, such as nausea, sweating, shakiness, and anxiety after stopping drinking
    4. Tolerance—The need to drink greater amounts of alcohol to get "high"
  - Alcoholism runs in families.
  - Genes play a role in transmitting the disease, but other factors—such as lifestyle and stress—contribute to a person's risk of becoming alcoholic.
  - Not every child of an alcoholic becomes an alcoholic; conversely, people with no family history of alcoholism can become alcoholics.
  - Alcoholism cannot be cured, but it can be effectively treated with counseling and medication.
- A person can abuse alcohol without becoming an alcoholic: They may drink too much and experience problems with alcohol without actually becoming physically dependent on alcohol.

- Some of the problems linked to alcohol abuse include not being able to meet work, school, or family responsibilities, drunk-driving arrests and car crashes, and drinking-related medical conditions.
- Under some circumstances, even social or moderate drinking is dangerous—for example, when driving, during pregnancy, or when taking certain medications.
- Nearly 14 million people in the United States—one in every thirteen adults—abuse alcohol or are alcoholic.
- In general, more men than women are alcohol dependent or have alcohol problems. Alcohol problems are highest among young adults between ages eighteen and twenty-nine and lowest among adults ages sixty-five and older.
- People who start drinking at an early age—for example, at age fourteen or younger—greatly increase the chance that they will develop alcohol problems at some point in their lives.

Acceptable and Unacceptable Drinking

- For most adults, moderate alcohol use—up to two drinks per day for men and one drink per day for women and older people—causes few if any problems. (One drink equals one twelve-ounce bottle of beer or wine cooler, one five-ounce glass of wine, or one and one-half ounces of eighty-proof distilled spirits.)
- Certain people should not drink at all, however:
  - Women who are pregnant or trying to become pregnant
  - People who plan to drive or engage in other activities that require alertness and skill (such as using high-speed machinery)
  - People taking certain over-the-counter or prescription medications
  - People with medical conditions that can be made worse by drinking
  - Recovering alcoholics
  - People younger than age twenty-one.

Evaluating Someone's Drinking

- Answering the following four questions can help you find out if you or a loved one has a drinking problem:
  1. Have you ever felt you should cut down on your drinking?
  2. Have people annoyed you by criticizing your drinking?

3. Have you ever felt bad or guilty about your drinking?
4. Have you ever had a drink first thing in the morning to steady your nerves or to get rid of a hangover?

One "yes" answer suggests a possible alcohol problem. More than one "yes" answer means it is highly likely that a problem exists. If you think that you or someone you know might have an alcohol problem, it is important to see a doctor or other health care provider right away.

The Health Effects of Alcohol

- Moderate drinkers—men who have two or less drinks per day and women who have one or less drinks per day—are less likely to die from one form of heart disease than are people who do not drink any alcohol or who drink more. It is believed that these smaller amounts of alcohol help protect against heart disease by changing the blood's chemistry, thus reducing the risk of blood clots in the heart's arteries.
- Heavy drinking can actually increase the risk of heart failure, stroke, and high blood pressure, as well as cause many other medical problems, such as liver cirrhosis.

Rates of Alcohol Use

- The U.S. Substance Abuse and Mental Health Services Administration, a division of the Department of Health and Human Services, provides the following statistics from a 2003 survey on alcohol use in the United States:
  - About half of Americans aged twelve or older reported being current drinkers of alcohol. This translates to an estimated 119 million people.
  - More than one-fifth (22.6 percent) of persons aged twelve or older participated in binge drinking at least once in the past thirty days. This translates to about 54 million people.
  - In 2003, heavy drinking was reported by 6.8 percent of the population aged twelve or older, or 16.1 million people.
  - Among young people, the prevalence of current alcohol use in 2003 increased with age, from 2.9 percent at age twelve to about 70 percent of persons twenty-one or twenty-two years old. Among older age groups, the prevalence of alcohol use decreased with increasing age, from 61.7 percent among twenty-six- to

twenty-nine-year-olds to 46.2 percent among sixty- to sixty-four-year-olds and 34.4 percent among people aged sixty-five or older.

Gender
- In general, males were more likely than females to report past month alcohol use. In 2003, 57.3 percent of males aged twelve or older were current drinkers compared with 43.2 percent of females. However, for the youngest age group (twelve to seventeen), the rates were not significantly different (17.1 percent for males vs. 18.3 percent for females).
- Among adults aged eighteen or older, 62.4 percent of males reported current and 46.0 percent of adult females reported current alcohol use in 2003.

Race/Ethnicity
- Whites were more likely than any other racial/ethnic group to report current use of alcohol in 2003. An estimated 54.4 percent of whites reported past month use. The rates were 44.4 percent for persons reporting two or more races, 43.3 percent for Native Hawaiians or Other Pacific Islanders, 42.0 percent for American Indians or Alaska Natives, 41.5 percent for Hispanics, 39.8 percent for Asians, and 37.9 percent for blacks.
- The rate of binge alcohol use was lowest among Asians (11.0 percent). Rates for other racial/ethnic groups were 19.0 percent for blacks, 23.6 percent for whites, 24.2 percent for Hispanics, 29.6 percent for American Indians/Alaska Natives, and 29.8 percent for Native Hawaiians or Other Pacific Islanders.
- Among youths aged twelve to seventeen in 2003, blacks and Asians were least likely to report past month alcohol use. Only 8.7 percent of Asian youths and 10.1 percent of black youths were current drinkers, while rates were above 15 percent for other racial/ethnic groups.

Underage Drinking
The NIAAA reports the following statistics on underage drinking in the United States:

- Alcohol is the number one drug of choice among children and adolescents. A higher percentage of youth between twelve and twenty use alcohol (29.0 percent) than use tobacco (23.3 percent) or illicit drugs.

- In 2002, about 2 million youth ages twelve through twenty drank five or more drinks on an occasion five or more times a month, and more than 7 million reported this level of consumption at least once in the survey month.
- Alcohol use by persons under age twenty-one poses both short-term and long-term risks:
  - In 2002, 1.5 million youth ages twelve through seventeen were in need of alcohol treatment. Of these, only 120,000 received treatment.
  - Alcohol is the leading cause of death for persons under age twenty-one.
  - Each year about nineteen hundred persons under twenty-one die in motor vehicle crashes that involve underage drinking.
  - Alcohol is also involved in about sixteen hundred homicides and three hundred suicides among persons under age twenty-one.
  - About sixteen hundred persons under age twenty-one die from alcohol-related unintentional injuries (not related to motor vehicle crashes).
  - Forty percent of those who start drinking before the age of fifteen become dependent on alcohol at some point in their lives.
  - Research indicates that the human brain continues to develop into a person's early twenties and that exposure of the developing brain to alcohol may have long-lasting effects on intellectual capabilities and may increase the likelihood of alcohol addiction.

The following statistics come from the 2003 SAMHSA survey:
- In the 2003 survey, about 10.9 million persons aged twelve to twenty reported drinking alcohol in the past month (29.0 percent of this age group). Nearly 7.2 million (19.2 percent) were binge drinkers, and 2.3 million (6.1 percent) were heavy drinkers.
- More males than females aged twelve to twenty reported binge drinking (21.7 vs. 16.5 percent) and heavy drinking (7.9 vs. 4.3 percent) in 2003.
- Among persons aged twelve to twenty, past month alcohol use rates ranged from 18.2 percent among Asians and blacks to 33.2 percent for whites. Binge drinking was reported by 22.8 percent of underage whites, 20.8 percent of underage American Indians or Alaska Natives, and 16.9 percent of underage Hispanics, but only by 9.6 percent of underage Asians and 9.1 percent of underage blacks.

ORGANIZATIONS TO CONTACT

The editors have compiled the following list of organizations concerned with the issues debated in this book. The descriptions are derived from materials provided by the organizations. All have publications or information available for interested readers. The list was compiled on the date of publication of the present volume; the information provided here may change. Be aware that many organizations take several weeks or longer to respond to inquiries, so allow as much time as possible.

Al-Anon Family Group Headquarters
1600 Corporate Landing Pkwy., Virginia Beach, VA 23454
(757) 563-1600
fax: (757) 563-1655
Web site: www.al-anon.alateen.org

Al-Anon is a fellowship of men, women, and children whose lives have been affected by an alcoholic family member or friend. Members share their experiences, strength, and hope to help each other and perhaps to aid in the recovery of the alcoholic. Al-Anon Family Group Headquarters provides information on its local chapters and on its affiliated organization, Alateen. Its publications include the monthly magazine the *Forum,* the semiannual *Al-Anon Speaks Out,* the bimonthly *Alateen Talk,* and several books, including *How Al-Anon Works, Path to Recovery: Steps, Traditions, and Concepts,* and *Courage to Be Me: Living with Alcoholism.*

Alcohol Advisory Council of New Zealand (ALAC)
Level 13, Castrol House, 36 Customhouse Quay, PO Box 5023, Wellington, New South Wales, New Zealand
04-917-0600
fax: 04-473-0890
e-mail: central@alac.org.nz
Web site: www.alcohol.org.nz

The Alcohol Advisory Council of New Zealand's primary objective is to promote moderation in the use of alcohol and develop and promote strategies that will reduce alcohol problems for the nation. ALAC has a Maori Unit that coordinates initiatives to reduce alcohol-related harm for the Maori. The organization publishes a quarterly newsletter in addition to research reports and government studies. All publications are available on the Web site.

Alcoholics Anonymous (AA)
General Service Office, PO Box 459, Grand Central Station,
New York, NY 10163
(212) 870-3400
fax: (212) 870-3003
Web site: www.aa.org

Alcoholics Anonymous is an international fellowship of people who are recovering from alcoholism. Because AA's primary goal is to help alcoholics remain sober, it does not sponsor research or engage in education about alcoholism. AA does, however, publish a catalog of literature concerning the organization as well as several pamphlets, including *Is AA for You? Young People and AA* and *A Brief Guide to Alcoholics Anonymous.*

American Beverage Institute (ABI)
1775 Pennsylvania Ave. NW, Suite 1200, Washington, DC 20006
(202) 463-7110
Web site: www.abionline.org

The American Beverage Institute is a restaurant industry trade organization that works to protect the consumption of alcoholic beverages in the restaurant setting. It unites wine, beer, and spirits producers with distributors and on-premise retailers in this effort. ABI conducts research and education in an attempt to demonstrate that the vast majority of adults who drink alcohol outside of the home are responsible, law-abiding citizens. Its Web site includes fact sheets, news articles, and research reports, including *The Anti-Drunk Driving Campaign: A Covert War Against Drinking* and *The .08 Debate: What's the Harm?*

The Beer Institute
122 C St. NW, Suite 750, Washington, DC 20001
(202) 737-2337
e-mail: info@beerinstitute.org
Web site: www.beerinstitute.org

The Beer Institute is a trade organization that represents the beer industry before Congress, state legislatures, and public forums across the country. It sponsors educational programs to prevent underage drinking and drunk driving and distributes fact sheets and news briefs on issues such as alcohol taxes and advertising. Its Issue Backrounder "Beer Advertising Facts" can be found on its Web site, and its *Beer Institute Bulletin* newsletter is published four times a year.

Canadian Centre on Substance Abuse/Centre canadien de lutte contre l'alcoolisme et les toxicomanies (CCSA/CCLAT)
75 Albert St., Suite 300, Ottawa, ON K1P 5E7 Canada
(613) 235-4048
fax: (613) 235-8101
Web site: www.ccsa.ca

A Canadian clearinghouse on substance abuse, the CCSA/CCLAT works to disseminate information on the nature, extent, and consequences of substance abuse and to support and assist organizations involved in substance abuse treatment, prevention, and educational programming. The CCSA/CCLAT publishes several books, including *Canadian Profile: Alcohol, Tobacco, and Other Drugs,* as well as reports, policy documents, brochures, research papers, and the newsletter *Action News.*

Center for Science in the Public Interest (CSPI)
1875 Connecticut Ave. NW, Suite 300, Washington, DC 20009
(202) 332-9110
fax: (202) 265-4954
e-mail: cspi@cspinet.org
Web site: www.cspinet.org

The center is an advocacy organization that promotes nutrition and health, food safety, alcohol policy, and sound science. It favors the implementation of public policies aimed at reducing alcohol-related problems, such as restricting alcohol advertising and increasing alcohol taxes. CSPI publishes the monthly *Nutrition Action Healthletter,* and its Web site contains fact sheets and reports on alcohol-related problems and policies, including the policy paper "Alcohol Advertising: Are Our Kids Collateral or Intended Targets?"

Center on Alcohol Marketing and Youth (CAMY)
2233 Wisconsin Ave. NW, Suite 525, Washington, DC 20007
(202) 687-1019
e-mail: info@camy.org
Web site: www.camy.org

The Center on Alcohol Marketing and Youth at Georgetown University is a nonprofit organization that monitors the marketing practices of the alcohol industry to focus attention and action on industry practices that it believes jeopardize the health and safety of America's youth. It seeks to reduce underage alcohol consumption by limiting the access to and appeal of alcohol to underage persons. CAMY publishes fact sheets and reports, including "Alcohol Advertising on Television, 2001 to 2003: More of the Same" and "Clicking with Kids: Alcohol Marketing and Youth on the Internet."

Centre for Addiction and Mental Health/Centre de toxicomanie at de sante' mentale (CAMH)
33 Russell St., Toronto, ON M5S 2S1 Canada
(416) 535-8501
Web site: www.camh.net

CAMH is a public hospital and the largest addiction facility in Canada. It also functions as a research facility, an education and training center, and a community-based organization providing health and addiction prevention services throughout Ontario, Canada. Further, CAMH is a Pan American Health Organization and World Health Organization Collaborating Centre. CAMH publishes the quarterly *CrossCurrents, the Journal of Addiction and Mental Health* and offers free alcoholism prevention literature that can be downloaded or ordered on the Web site.

Century Council
1310 G St. NW, Suite 600, Washington, DC 20005
(202) 637-0077
fax: (202) 637-0079
e-mail: kimballl@centurycouncil.org
Web site: www.centurycouncil.org

A nonprofit organization funded by America's liquor industry, the Century Council's mission is to fight drunk driving and underage drinking. It seeks to promote responsible decision making about drinking and discourage all forms of irresponsible alcohol consumption through education, communication, research, law enforcement, and other programs. Its Web site offers fact sheets and other resources on drunk driving, underage drinking, and other alcohol-related problems.

Distilled Spirits Council of the United States (DISCUS)
1250 I St. NW, Suite 900, Washington, DC 20005
(202) 628-3544
Web site: www.discus.org

The Distilled Spirits Council of the United States is the national trade association representing producers and marketers of distilled spirits in the United States. It seeks to ensure the responsible advertising and marketing of distilled spirits to adult consumers and to prevent such advertising and marketing from targeting individuals below the legal purchase age. DISCUS publishes fact sheets, news releases, and documents, including its "Code of Responsible Practices for Beverage Alcohol Advertising and Marketing."

International Center for Alcohol Policies (ICAP)
1519 New Hampshire Ave. NW, Washington, DC 20036
(202) 986-1159
fax: (202) 986-2080
Web site: www.icap.org

The International Center for Alcohol Policies is a nonprofit organization dedicated to helping reduce the abuse of alcohol worldwide and to promoting understanding of the role of alcohol in society through dialogue and partnerships involving the beverage industry, the public health community, and others interested in alcohol policy. ICAP is supported by eleven major international beverage alcohol companies. ICAP publishes reports on pertinent issues such as *Safe Alcohol Consumption, The Limits of Binge Drinking, Health Warning Labels, Drinking Age Limits, What Is a "Standard Drink"?, Government Policies on Alcohol and Pregnancy, Estimating Costs Associated with Alcohol Abuse,* and *Who Are the Abstainers?*

The Marin Institute
24 Belvedere St., San Rafael, CA 94901
(415) 456-5692
Web site: www.marininstitute.org

The Marin Institute works to reduce alcohol problems by improving the physical and social environment to advance public health and safety. The institute promotes stricter alcohol policies—including higher taxes—in order to reduce alcohol-related problems. It publishes fact sheets and news alerts on alcohol policy, advertising, and other alcohol-related issues. Its "Talk Back System" allows users of its Web site to complain directly to the alcohol industry about irresponsible advertising and marketing practices.

Mothers Against Drunk Driving (MADD)
511 E. John Carpenter Fwy., No. 700, Irving, TX 75062
800-GET-MADD (438-6233)
fax: (972) 869-2206/07
e-mail: Information: info@madd.org
e-mail: Victim's Assistance: victims@madd.org
Web site: www.madd.org

Mothers Against Drunk Driving seeks to act as the voice of victims of drunk-driving accidents by speaking on their behalf to communities, businesses, and educational groups and by providing materials for use in medical facilities and health and driver education programs. MADD publishes the biannual *MADDvocate for Victims Magazine* and the newsletter *MADD in Action* as well as a variety of fact sheets, brochures, and other materials on drunk driving.

National Center on Addiction and Substance Abuse (CASA)
633 Third Ave., 19th Floor, New York, NY 10017-6706
(212) 841-5200
Web site: www.casacolumbia.org

CASA is a nonprofit organization affiliated with Columbia University. It works to educate the public about the problems of substance abuse and addiction and evaluate prevention, treatment, and law enforcement programs to address the problem. Its Web site contains reports and op-ed articles on alcohol policy and the alcohol industry, including the reports

Teen Tipplers: America's Underage Drinking Epidemic and *The Economic Value of Underage and Adult Excessive Drinking to the Alcohol Industry.*

National Council on Alcoholism and Drug Dependence (NCADD)
20 Exchange Pl., Suite 2902, New York, NY 10005
(212) 269-7797
fax: (212) 269-7510
Hope line: (800) 622-2255
Web site: www.ncadd.org

NCADD is a volunteer health organization that helps individuals overcome addictions, advises the federal government on drug and alcohol policies, and develops substance abuse prevention and education programs for youth. It publishes fact sheets, such as *Youth and Alcohol,* and pamphlets, such as *Who's Got the Power? You . . . or Drugs?*

National Highway Traffic Safety Administration (NHTSA)
400 Seventh St. SW, Washington, DC 20590
(888) 327-4236
Web site: www.nhtsa.dot.gov

The NHTSA is a department of the U.S. Department of Transportation that is responsible for reducing deaths, injuries, and economic losses resulting from motor vehicle crashes. It sets and enforces safety performance standards for motor vehicles and motor vehicle equipment and awards grants to state and local governments to enable them to conduct local highway safety programs. The NHTSA publishes information on drunk driving, including *Get the Keys* and *Strategies for Success: Combating Juvenile DUI.*

National Institute on Alcohol Abuse and Alcoholism (NIAAA)
5635 Fishers Ln., MSC 9304, Bethesda, MD 20892-9304
(301) 496-4000
Web site: www.niaaa.nih.gov

The National Institute on Alcoholism and Alcohol Abuse is one of the eighteen institutes that comprise the National Institutes of Health. NIAAA provides leadership in the national effort to reduce alcohol-related problems. It publishes the quarterly bulletin *Alcohol Alert,* the quarterly scientific journal *Alcohol Research and Health,* and many pamphlets, brochures, and posters dealing with alcohol abuse and alcoholism. All of these publications including NIAAA's congressional testimony are available online.

National Organization on Fetal Alcohol Syndrome (NOFAS)
900 Seventeenth St. NW, Suite 910, Washington, DC 20006
(202) 785-4585
(800) 66 NOFAS
fax: (202) 466-6456
e-mail: information@nofas.org
Web site: www.nofas.org

NOFAS is a nonprofit organization dedicated to eliminating birth defects caused by alcohol consumption during pregnancy and improving the quality of life for those individuals and families affected. The organization sponsors many outreach and educational programs and publishes a quarterly newsletter, *Notes from NOFAS,* in addition to many fact sheets and brochures. Some information is available online. An information packet can be ordered through the mail.

Rational Recovery Systems (RRS)
PO Box 800, Lotus, CA 95651
(530) 621-2667
(530) 621-4374
e-mail: rrsn@rational.org
Web site: www.rational.org/recovery

RRS is a national self-help organization that offers a cognitive rather than spiritual approach to recovery from alcoholism. Its philosophy holds that alcoholics can attain sobriety without depending on other people or a "higher power." Rational Recovery Systems publishes materials about the organization and its use of rational-emotive therapy.

Research Society on Alcoholism (RSA)
7801 N. Lamar Blvd., Suite D-89, Austin, TX 78752-1038
(512) 454-0022
fax: (512) 454-0812
e-mail: debbyrsa@bga.com
Web site: www.rsoa.org

The RSA provides a forum for researchers who share common interests in alcoholism. The society's purpose is to promote research on the prevention and treatment of alcoholism. It publishes the journal *Alcoholism: Clinical and Experimental Research* nine times a year as well as the book series Recent Advances in Alcoholism.

Secular Organizations for Sobriety (SOS)
4773 Hollywood Blvd., Hollywood, CA 90027
(323) 666-4295
e-mail: SOS@CFIWest.org
Web sites: www.secularsobriety.org

SOS is a network of groups dedicated to helping individuals achieve and maintain sobriety. Its members believe that alcoholics can best recover by rationally choosing to make sobriety rather than alcohol a priority. Most members of SOS reject the spiritual basis of Alcoholics Anonymous and other similar self-help groups. SOS publishes the quarterly *SOS International Newsletter* and distributes the books *Unhooked: Staying Sober and Drug Free* and *How to Stay Sober: Recovery Without Religion,* written by SOS founder James Christopher.

Substance Abuse and Mental Health Services Administration (SAMHSA)
National Clearinghouse for Alcohol and Drug Information (NCADI)
PO Box 2345, Rockville, MD 20847-2345
(800) 729-6686 • (301) 468-2600
TDD: (800) 487-4889
fax: (301) 230-2867
Web site: www.health.org

SAMHSA is a division of the U.S. Department of Health and Human Services that is responsible for improving the lives of those with or at risk for mental illness or substance addiction. Through the NCADI, SAMHSA provides the public with a wide variety of information on alcoholism and other addictions. Its publications include the bimonthly *Prevention Pipeline,* the fact sheet *Alcohol Alert,* monographs such as "Social Marketing/Media Advocacy" and "Advertising and Alcohol," brochures, pamphlets, videotapes, and posters. Publications in Spanish are also available.

Books

Anatoly Antoshechkin, *Alcohol: Poison or Medicine?* Bloomington, IN: 1st Books Library, 2002. Offers new scientific data showing that alcohol in moderate doses reduces stress, depression, and the risk of heart disease and type 2 diabetes while increasing the drinker's lifespan.

Griffith Edwards, *Alcohol: The World's Favorite Drug.* New York: Thomas Dunne Books, 2002. Discusses the social and medical problems associated with alcohol and the history of treatment methods. Covers the temperance movement, Prohibition, Alcoholics Anonymous, and a range of contemporary issues.

Kathleen Whalen Fitzgerald, *Alcoholism: The Genetic Inheritance.* Friday Harbor, WA: Whales' Tales Press, 2002. Written by a recovering alcoholic and novelist, this volume presents the argument that alcoholism is an inheritable disease. It also offers advice for alcoholics and the family members of alcoholics.

Anne M. Fletcher, *Sober for Good: New Solutions for Drinking Problems—Advice from Those Who Have Succeeded.* Boston: Houghton Mifflin, 2002. Presents the stories of many people who have overcome drinking problems in various ways—most of them without the help of Alcoholics Anonymous.

Gene Ford, *The Science of Healthy Drinking.* San Francisco: Wine Appreciation Guild, 2003. A researcher and expert on drinking and health presents the evidence that moderate drinking is beneficial to human health. He even found that moderate drinkers have a higher income.

Dwight B. Heath, *Drinking Occasions: Comparative Perspectives on Alcohol and Culture.* New York: Brunner-Routledge, 2000. An anthropology professor describes the many ways that alcohol is used responsibly and with positive results in cultures around the world.

Katherine Ketchum et al., *Beyond the Influence: Understanding and Defeating Alcoholism.* New York: Bantam Dell, 2000. Presents the argument that alcoholism is a disease of the body rather than a character flaw. Also provides information on the diagnosis and treatment of alcoholism.

Jodee Kulp, *The Best I Can Be: Living with Fetal Alcohol Syndrome.* St. Paul, MN: Better Endings, New Beginnings, 2000. A teen describes what it is like to live with fetal alcohol syndrome.

Robert S. Lazich, *Alcohol and Tobacco: America's Drugs of Choice.* Detroit: Information Plus, 2004. A thorough reference book with general information and statistics on alcohol. Chapters examine the extent and effects of alcohol use, alcohol abuse and addiction, and youth alcohol use.

Eric Newhouse, *Alcohol: Cradle to Grave.* Center City, MN: Hazelden Information Education, 2001. A journalistic look at the social costs of alcoholism in a Montana town.

J. Vincent Peterson, Bernard Nisenholz, and Gary T. Robinson, *A Nation Under the Influence: America's Addiction to Alcohol.* Boston: Allyn and Bacon, 2002. An overview of alcohol abuse and alcoholism in American society that offers a historical perspective as well as coverage of contemporary issues, including prevention and treatment, advertising, and underage drinking.

Bert Pluymen, *The Thinking Person's Guide to Sobriety.* New York: Griffin Trade Paperbacks, 2000. Writing in a humorous style, the author tells the story of how he overcame his alcoholism and offers advice to others facing the same situation.

C.K. Robertson, ed., *Religion and Alcohol: Sobering Thoughts.* New York: P. Lang, 2004. A collection of ten essays that explore attitudes toward drinking in various religious traditions, including Christianity, Islam, and Judaism.

Sarah W. Tracy and Caroline Jean Acker, eds., *Altering American Consciousness: The History of Alcohol and Drug Use in the United States, 1800–2000.* Amherst: University of Massachusetts Press, 2004. An anthology of articles on the history of drug and alcohol use in America with a particular focus on how social and cultural changes have affected the use and acceptability of different substances at different times.

Henry Wechsler and Bernice Wuethrich, *Dying to Drink: Confronting Binge Drinking on College Campuses.* Emmaus, PA: Rodale Press, 2002. Describes the extent of binge drinking on college campuses and the problems associated with this behavior, such as its impact on crime.

The authors also offer recommendations for reducing the rate of college drinking.

Periodicals and Reports

Radley Balko, "A Toast to the Holiday?" *Washington Times,* January 1, 2004.

Susan Brink, "When Being First Isn't Best," *U.S. News & World Report,* May 7, 2001.

———, "Your Brain on Alcohol," *U.S. News & World Report,* May 7, 2001.

Joseph A. Califano Jr., "Don't Make Teen Drinking Easier," *Washington Post,* May 11, 2003.

Ira Carnahan, "Sober Up," *Forbes,* July 26, 2004.

Center on Alcohol Marketing and Youth, *Alcohol Advertising on Television, 2001 to 2003: More of the Same,* Washington, DC, October 12, 2004.

———, *Clicking with Kids: Alcohol Marketing and Youth on the Internet,* Washington, DC, March 2004.

Barbara Ehrenreich, "Libation as Liberation? Going Toe to Toe with Men Is a Feminist Act; Going Drink for Drink with Them Isn't," *Time,* April 1, 2002.

Jim Gogek, "Putting Caps on Teenage Drinking," *New York Times,* August 25, 2004.

Paul Gruenewald and Robert Saltz, "College Drinking Is Not a Given," *Christian Science Monitor,* December 14, 2004.

David J. Hanson, "Age of Propaganda: The Government Attacks Teenage Drinking with Junk Science," *Reason,* October 2004.

Collin Levey, "Lame Lawsuits and Spirit of the Season!" *Seattle Times,* January 1, 2004.

Joshua A. Levine, "Get Real About Teenage Drinking," *Boston Globe,* November 20, 2004.

Steven Milloy, "Alcohol Report Anomaly," *Washington Times,* September 30, 2003.

Jodie Morse, "Women on a Binge: Many Teen Girls Are Drinking as Much as Boys," *Time,* April 1, 2002.

Mothers Against Drunk Driving, *It's Time to Get MADD All Over Again: Resuscitating the Nation's Efforts to Prevent Impaired Driving,* Irving, TX, June 2002.

National Center on Addiction and Substance Abuse, *Teen Tipplers: America's Underage Drinking Epidemic,* rev. ed., New York, February 2003.

National Highway Traffic Safety Administration, *Initiatives to Address Impaired Driving,* Washington, DC, December 2003.

National Research Council and the Institute of Medicine, *Reducing Underage Drinking: A Collective Responsibility,* Washington, DC, National Academies Press, 2004.

Hans Nichols, "Getting Drunk on Rebellion," *Insight,* July 16, 2001.

Dennis Prager, "Jenna Bush Is Old Enough to Drink," *Wall Street Journal,* June 8, 2001.

Ed Quillen, "The Logic of Responsibility," *Denver Post,* September 26, 2004.

R.T. Reid, "Let My Teenager Drink," *Washington Post,* May 4, 2003.

Lucille Roybal-Allard, "Illegal Underage Drinking Is a National Health Crisis, and Congress Must Enact a National Strategy to Fight It Effectively," *Insight,* October 27, 2003.

San Francisco Chronicle, "Alcohol's Allure," April 6, 2003.

Karen Springen and Barbara Kantrowitz, "Alcohol's Deadly Triple Threat: Women Get Addicted Faster, Seek Help Less Often, and Are More Likely to Die from the Bottle," *Newsweek,* May 10, 2004.

Michael Steel, "A Hearty Booze Battle," *National Journal,* June 9, 2001.

Gary Stix, "Should Physicians Tell Some Nondrinkers to Start?" *Scientific American,* July 17, 2001.

Steven Stocker, "Finding the Future Alcoholic," *Futurist,* May 2002.

Jamie Talan, "The Search for Genetic Keys to Alcoholism," *Los Angeles Times,* May 21, 2001.

U.S. Federal Trade Commission, *Alcohol Marketing and Advertising: A Report to Congress,* Washington, DC, September 2003.

U.S. General Accounting Office, *Report to Congressional Committees: Highway Safety: Effectiveness of State .08 Blood Alcohol Content Laws,* Washington, DC, June 1999.

Web Sites

Alcohol: Problems and Solutions (www2.potsdam.edu/alcohol-info). This site is hosted by David J. Hanson, a professor emeritus of sociology at the State University of New York at Potsdam who has studied alcohol and drinking for more than thirty years. The site contains many articles that express Hanson's stance on alcohol-related issues, including the health benefits of alcohol, minimum drinking-age laws, and alcohol advertising.

Drink Smart (www.drinksmart.orgw). Drink Smart is a Canadian-based electronic magazine that promotes the responsible consumption of alcohol. It publishes personal stories on drinking and driving, the effects of alcohol on families, and attitudes toward drinking among teens and at colleges.

Indiana University, Bloomington, Alcohol Research and Health Information (www.indiana.edu/~engs/index.shtml). This site provides the text of numerous studies on binge drinking, the minimum drinking age, and the health affects of alcohol.

Lowe Family Foundation (www.lowefamily.org). The Lowe Family Foundation is a charity organization dedicated to providing assistance to people coping with alcohol abuse in their family. The Web site includes interviews with experts on alcohol abuse and a comprehensive listing of alcohol and drug abuse counseling organizations nationwide.

Stanton Peele's Addiction Website (www.peele.net). Stanton Peele is a New Jersey lawyer and psychologist who has been studying addiction for thirty years. He rejects the view that alcoholism is a disease and that abstinence is the only treatment for alcohol abuse. His Web site contains information and articles that express his views, some of which are controversial.

Teen Advice Online (TAO) (www.teenadviceonline.org) TAO's teen counselors from around the world offer advice for teens on substance abuse as well as relationships, dating, sex, and other issues. Teens can submit questions to the counselors or read about similar problems in the archives.

on alcohol deaths and drinking
age, 100
on underage drinking, 17–18, 80
Chapman, Steven, 98
Churchill, Winston, 22
college drinking
consequences of, 47–48
as a culture, 46–47
extreme forms of, 51
prevalence of, 48
studies on, are flawed, 53–54
Congress, U.S.
actions against underage drinking
by, 31
attempts to raise alcohol taxes by,
67
on blood alcohol concentration
limits, 111–12
on legal drinking age, 98, 106
Conners, Gerald, 19
Coors, Peter, 100
crime, college drinking and, 47–48

Daily Telegraph (newspaper), 24
Davis, Gray, 63
deaths, alcohol-related, 55
among college students, 46
in drunk-driving cases, driver
blood alcohol content and, 119
effects of minimum-age drinking
laws on, 100–101
low blood alcohol content laws
do not reduce, 117
among youth, 80–82
Department of Health and Human
Services, U.S. (USDHHS), 29,
50
Doyle, John, 109
Drinking: A Love Story (Knapp), 15
*Drinking Occasions: Comparative
Perspectives on Alcohol and
Culture* (Heath), 25

drunk driving
among college students, 48
low blood alcohol content laws
do not reduce, 117
see also accidents, drunk driving

Economist (magazine), 100, 103
Education Health (magazine), 40
elderly, alcohol abuse among,
19–20
Engels, Rutger C.M.E., 39

Federal Trade Commission (FTC),
31, 93–95
Foster, Sue, 37
Frederick the Great, 25

Gallagher, Christine, 16
Gallagher, Dick, 16
Gillespie, Nick, 34
Gogek, Jim, 59
Goldberg, Ira J., 19
Goldman, Mark, 56
Government Accounting Office
(GAO), 65

Hacker, George, 17
Hamilton, Wendy, 119–20
Hammer, T., 43
Hartman, B.R., 43
Harvard School of Public Health, 48
health
benefits of alcohol to, 11
college drinking and, 48
effects of alcohol abuse on, 20
Healthy People 2010 (U.S. govern-
ment report), 50
Heath, Dwight D., 25
Hingson, Ralph, 53, 56, 57, 76
Hurley, Chuck, 101

injuries, from college drinking, 46

PICTURE CREDITS

Cover: Photos.com
AP/WideWorld Photos, 18, 23, 29, 35, 49, 54, 56, 67, 80, 85, 105
© Paul Barton/CORBIS, 93
Brand X Pictures/Getty Images, 41
Matt Campbell/EPA/Landov, 99
Hans Ericsson/EPA/Landov, 10
Chris Hondros/Getty Images, 69
© Hutchings Stock Photography/CORBIS, 97
© Catherine Karnow/CORBIS, 11
Michael Kleinfeld/UPI/Landov, 66
Frank May/EPA/Landov, 58
Darren McCollester/Getty Images, 61
David McNew/Getty Images, 30
Mike Mergern/Bloomberg News/Landov, 91
© Roy Morsch/CORBIS, 95
George Nikitin/EPA/Landov, 62
Fredrik Persson/AFP/Getty Images, 13
© Mark Peterson/CORBIS, 73, 118
PhotoDisc, 102, 114
Photos.com, 43, 60
Reuters/Landov, 15
© Royalty-Free/CORBIS, 42
Sue Santillan, 28, 37, 50, 74, 79, 81, 101, 112
© Shepard Sherbell/CORBIS SABA, 106
© F. Carter Smith/CORBIS SYGMA, 88
Justin Sullivan/Getty Images, 55, 111
Alex Wong/Getty Images, 120
© Lacassagne Xavier/CORBIS SYGMA, 36
Rungroj Yongrit/EPA/Landov, 9

ABOUT THE EDITOR

Scott Barbour received a bachelor's degree in English and a master's degree in social work from San Diego State University. He has worked as a case manager and counselor with the severely mentally ill. He is currently a senior acquisitions editor for Greenhaven Press, for whom he has edited numerous books on social issues, historical topics, and current events.